THE SEARCH FOR A COLD WAR GRAND STRATEGY

ABSTRACT

THE SEARCH FOR A COLD WAR GRAND STRATEGY: NSC 68 & 162, BY COL CRAIG BERRYMAN, U.S. ARMY, 81 PAGES.

The Soviet Union's behavior following the conclusion of World War II challenged United States policy. Communist aggression around the world created a turbulent and difficult environment for the United States and Western Europe to address. Communist actions increased the difficulties for the United States which simultaneously attempted to stabilize the global economy and Western European governments. U.S. policy lacked focus and senior leaders urged President Harry S. Truman to review national policy. The political environment following the conclusion of World War II was not optimal for President Truman to request an increase in the U.S. military budget. The North Korean attack on South Korea gave impetus to an invigorated national defense policy. The attack justified an increase in defense spending in support of NSC 68 policy recommendations. President Dwight D. Eisenhower assumed responsibility for a coherent national strategy after his successful election following President Harry S. Truman. President Eisenhower campaigned on a review of the national strategy as part of his promise for a "New Look." This study focuses on the creation and evolution of National Security Council policy recommendations by two distinctly different staffing procedures. It also identifies presidential and senior leadership experiences and influences of staff organizations that created successful national security policies. Their policy actions ultimately contributed to the successful collapse of the Union of Soviet Socialist Republics and degraded communism as a legitimate form of government in the late 1980s.

ACKNOWLEDGEMENTS

I would like to offer particular thanks to two Presidential Libraries and their research staff in assisting with this research project. My heartfelt thanks and gratitude to the Harry S. Truman Library archivists in Independence, Missouri and to the Dwight D. Eisenhower Library archivists in Abilene, Kansas. Your dedication and assistance made much of this research possible.

TABLE OF CONTENTS

ACRONYMS

AAF	Army Air Forces
ADM	Admiral
AEC	Atomic Energy Commission
CGSC	U.S. Army Command and General Staff College
CIA	Central Intelligence Agency
COA	Course of Action
DDEL	Dwight D. Eisenhower Library
FR	Foreign Relations
GNP	Gross National Product
LTG	Lieutenant General
MDMP	Military Decision Making Process
MG	Major General
MI	Military Intelligence
MSA	Mutual Security Agency
NATO	North Atlantic Treaty Organization
NIE	National Intelligence Estimate
NME	National Military Establishment
NSC	National Security Council
OSS	Office of Strategic Services
POLAD	Political Advisor
PPS	Policy Planning Staff
RADM	Rear Admiral
SecDef	Secretary of Defense
SHAEF	Supreme Headquarters Allied Expeditionary Force
SHAPE	Supreme Headquarters Allied Powers Europe
TF	Task Force

USA	United States Army
USAF	United States Air Force
USN	United States Navy
USSBS	United States Strategic Bombing Survey
VADM	Vice Admiral
WHOSANSA	White House Office of the Special Assistant for National Security Affairs Records, Eisenhower Library.
WHONSCS	White House Office, National Security Council Staff, Eisenhower Library.

INTRODUCTION

The Soviet Union, the United Kingdom and the United States successfully defeated Germany and Japan in 1945. The three victorious powers had discussed, planned and agreed upon the future of the new world order at the Yalta Conference in February of 1945 and again at the Potsdam Conference in July and August of 1945. The conferences were designed to establish a new post-war order, and mitigate the negative residual effects from a global world war. The Soviet Union did not behave as expected from the Yalta and Potsdam Conference agreements. The Soviets began to challenge the agreements established at Yalta and Potsdam.

Communist governments consolidated power and sought to influence or control peripheral countries. The Soviet Union internally consolidated their power. The Soviets aggressively advanced communism as the optimal form of government in the international realm. The U.S.S.R. became assertive and at times aggressive when dealing with neighboring countries. The Soviets opportunistically looked for countries that could be converted to communism. Communist China led by Mao Tse-Tung was in conflict with the Chinese Nationalist Party of Chiang Kai-shek. The communist movement appeared to be garnering strength. Pro-Communist elements loudly proclaimed and aggressively pushed communism as the form of governance which would legitimately lead the world.

American foreign policy searched for a way forward following the success of World War II.[1] The period reflected the ambivalence of an uncertain time. Communists and communism challenged American strategy and policy within a few short years. The Soviet Union attempted to seal off Berlin from West Germany. The United States attempted to lead Western Europe and

---

[1]The term policy will be used throughout this paper to serve as the overarching component that establishes, coordinates and integrates activities across various elements of strategic power. Policy for the purposes of this monograph will include strategy that integrates diplomatic, information, military and economic activities that seek to achieve a desired national objective.

1

toward a stable economic and social recovery. General Douglas MacArthur remained busy in Japan restructuring and re-establishing order within Japanese society. Leadership demands and pressures challenged American leadership. Wartime sacrifices resulted in a weary American society. America and her leaders were thrust into the spot light as the lead country of the free world.

Two United States presidents would set the stage for American foreign policy for the next thirty plus years. Presidents Harry S. Truman and Dwight D. Eisenhower set in motion a methodical and purposeful foreign policy. Their foreign policies were created and derived in two separate and distinct methods. The actions of both leaders and their subordinate staffs in the Department of State and the Department of Defense struggled to find the proper foreign policy balance. They would produce policies that would become recognized for charting a pronounced course of action. President Truman ultimately adopted the recommendations of National Security Council policy paper 68. President Eisenhower conducted the Solarium Exercise which contributed to National Security Council policy 162. These two National Security Council policies created the framework for how the United States would address and engage an aggressive Communist threat. The policies shaped how the United States would view and engage Russian leadership. Unfortunately neither of these two leaders had the opportunity to observe the fruit of their actions and policies. Both leaders successfully contributed to the collapse of functional communism governance in Eastern Europe in the 1990s.

This paper analyzes the development of National Security Council policies 68 and 162. The discussion of these two National Security Council policies provides insight into President Harry S. Truman and Dwight D. Eisenhower leadership styles, policy analysis, and influences of their staffs on the development of security policies to address the communist challenge. The development of both policies highlights the contributions of their respective advisors and staffs. The discussion and analysis highlights subordinate actions that influenced the development of a consistent, sound and thorough policy during this critical and challenging period of American and world history. Finally, the research project assesses the utility of these respective methods for future national security development.

PRESIDENT TRUMAN'S BASIC NATIONAL SECURITY POLICY, THE ATOMIC
QUESTION AND NSC 68

President Truman's Background

President Franklin Delano Roosevelt passed away April 12, 1945. Vice President Harry

S. Truman assumed the responsibilities as the President of the United States. President Roosevelt

did not keep Vice President Truman closely informed of his foreign policy plans or strategy.

President Roosevelt and Vice President Truman only met alone two times while in office

together.[2] President Truman assumed responsibility from a relatively "cold start."[3] In his first year

in office President Truman was thrust into the role of negotiator in chief at the Potsdam

Conference. President Truman made the momentous decision to employ atomic bombs against

Hiroshima and Nagasaki.

Several key events and Soviet actions that occurred during Truman's first presidential

tenure began to shape the geo-political landscape. President Truman authorized the atomic bomb

attacks on Hiroshima on 6 August, 1945 and on Nagasaki on 9 August, 1945. The Japanese

surrendered on 14 August, 1945 with a formal surrender ceremony 2 September, 1945. The

capabilities of the atomic bomb became known to the world and the Soviet Union took notice.

President Truman, like most Americans, hoped that the wartime cooperation with the

Soviet Union would carry on in the post-war world. A series of events, ranging from the Near

East to Central Europe eroded Truman's confidence in the two years following the end of the

war. The communists began to aggressively assert themselves. By 1947 suspicion was mounting

---

[2]Robert Dallek, *Harry S. Truman* (New York: Times Books, 2008), 16.

[3]Literature used to establish a background on Harry S. Truman and security challenges and policies include the following authors: Melvyn P. Leffler, *A Preponderance of Power. National Security, The Truman Administration, and the Cold War* (Stanford: Stanford University Press, 1992); Robert Dallek, *Harry S. Truman* (New York: Times Books, 2008); Ernest R. May, *American Cold War Strategy* (New York: Bedford Books of St. Martin's Press, 1993); John Lewis Gaddis, *Strategies of Containment, A Critical Appraisal of Postwar American National Security Policy* (New York: Oxford University Press, 1982).

in the U.S. government that policy towards the Soviet Union might need to be reappraised. The Soviet-backed coup in Czechoslovakia in March of 1948 raised a red flag concerning Soviet intentions. The Soviets then blocked the western sectors of Berlin on 24 June, 1948. The Berlin Airlift was initiated the following day. The Soviets lifted the ground blockade on May 11, 1949. These two significant events championed by the Soviets hardened opinion in capitals of Western Europe and in Washington, D.C.

The members of the nascent U.S. national security community began addressing the direction of U.S. foreign policy with the Soviet Union during World War II. Security analysts were asking questions about how the United States should address the Soviet Union. Analysts were seeking guidance and questioning what policies were needed to plan for future relations with the Soviets. George Kennan influenced the discussion of Soviet foreign policy in the summer of 1943. He served in the U.S. Embassy in Moscow and later became renowned for the 1946 "Long Telegram." The "Long Telegram" addressed the dangers of Soviet expansionism. Kennan's second influential work that highlighted Soviet actions and behaviors was discussed in the "Mr. X." article. The "Mr. X." article was published in the July 1947 *Foreign Affairs*. The Long Telegram and the Mr. X articles encapsulated much of the discussion about communist policy. The security discussions would ultimately produce a policy known as "containment." Containment recommended a policy that would limit Soviet power until "such time as the Soviet people awoke to the destruction of their heritage and withdrew their support from Stalinesque policies."[4]

While the policy of containment was in development George C. Marshall and the Department of State was developing a massive economic plan to aid Europe. George C. Marshall

---

[4]S. Nelson Drew, *NSC-68: Forging the Strategy of Containment with Analyses by Paul H. Nitze* (Washington, DC: National Defense University Press, 1994), 8.

was appointed as the 50th Secretary of State on January 21, 1947.[5] Secretary of State Marshall and the State Department developed the European Recovery Plan. The European Recovery Plan would famously become known as the Marshall Plan. The Marshall Plan was developed to facilitate the recovery of Europe and assist in modernizing the European economy. The Marshall Plan was not embraced by the Soviets and they restricted communist satellite countries from participating in the economic aid under the Marshall Plan.

The Truman administration had undertaken its first formal consideration of American *political* objectives in the event of war with the Soviet Union. The considerations of political objections were to counter objections of policy being conducted in a piecemeal process.[6] The National Military Establishment (NME) as part of the National Security Act of 1947. The NME was renamed the Department of Defense in 1949. The National Military Establishment was searching for greater clarity of objectives. The NME had consolidated all of the services and was responsible for recommending military options to support national security policy. The NME had responsibility for recommending force structure. It would be difficult for the NME to provide effective and calibrated recommendations to senior political leaders if the NME did not understand what potential threats they might have to respond to. The NME needed guidance to plan. Enhanced clarity would enable military leadership to provide refined options based on desired political objectives.

The resulting analysis and study of political objectives, drafted largely by George F. Kennan and the State Department Policy Planning Staff (PPS), concluded that the experience of World War II would not apply. The United States could not expect to achieve the unconditional

---

[5]U.S. Department of State, Office of the Historian, "Marshall, George Catlett," https://history.state.gov/departmenthistory/people/marshall-george-catlett (accessed 17 December 2013).

[6]Ernest R. May, *American Cold War Strategy* (New York: Bedford Books of St. Martin's Press, 1993), 4.

surrender of the Soviet government, or to impose its will upon the entire territory of the U.S.S.R. George Kennan and the Policy Planning Staff articulated to achieve an enduring solution to the tension between the Soviets and the United States, "We must recognize that whatever settlement we finally achieve must be a *political* settlement, *politically* negotiated."[7]

The National Security Council (NSC) released one of the first policies addressing Soviet Communism on 12 July 1948. NSC 20 was in response to a request from Secretary of Defense Forrestal. NSC 20 directed the "preparation of a statement which specifies and evaluates the risks of the future, states our objectives, and outlines measures to be followed in achieving them."[8] The final staffing resulted in NCS 20/4 becoming U.S. national security policy on 23 November, 1948.

Policy Planning Staff

The Secretary of State in 1948 was George C. Marshall. Marshall's experiences as Chief of Staff of the Army quickly led him to recognize that the State Department operated on a day to day tempo and addressed each crisis as the "crisis du jour." Marshall recognized that the State Department needed a separation between day to day activities and an element that was focused towards long term thinking and analysis. Secretary Marshall's State Department Policy Planning Staff was established to separate the broad array of current operations from long range planning. Secretary of State Marshall stated his appointment of George Kennan as the head of the newly created policy planning staff had a specific objective, "the point was to get him [Kennan] in there [Policy Planning]. I found out that there was nothing, no planning agency, at all. You can't plan

---

[7]See NSC 20/1, "U.S. Objectives with Respect to Russia," August 18, 1948 in Thomas H. Etzold and John Lewis Gaddis, eds., *Containment: Documents on American Policy and Strategy, 1945-1950* (New York: 1978), 193 and NSC 20/4, "U.S. Objectives with Respect to the U.S.S.R. to Counter Soviet Threats to U.S. Security," November 23, 1948, *Foreign Relations of the United States,* 1948: 1:667.

[8]Drew, 17.

and operate at the same [time]. They are two states of mind."[9] The separation of current

operations and planning enabled the Secretary of State to simultaneously focus on current actions

while planning for the future in detain with credible analysis. Dean Acheson later spoke of the

wisdom of splitting the functions, critically selecting the right person and the significance of

policies acquiring their own "life" when he recorded in his memoirs,

> [Secretary Marshall] conceived the function of this group as being to look ahead, not into the distant future, but beyond the vision of the operating officers caught in the smoke and crises of current battle; far enough ahead to see the emerging form of things to come and outline what should be done to meet or anticipate them. In doing this the staff should also do something else – constantly reappraise what was being done. General Marshall was acutely aware that policies acquired their own momentum and went on after the reasons that inspired them had ceased.[10]

The separation of operations and planning enabled the Secretary of State to better manage

immediate challenges while looking forward. This action facilitated long-range planning and

ensuring that current operations and planning were in accordance with policy. Finally, Secretary

Marshall established a mechanism to ensure assessment of current actions and policies were

better synchronized.

Secretary of State Marshall appointed George F. Kennan as the first director of the Policy

Planning Staff.[11] Kennan was considered the leading and rare specialist on the Soviet Union after

his time in the U.S. Embassy in Moscow. Kennan was recognized to be a premier expert who

really understood Soviet Union affairs. There were very few individuals who could rival

---

[9]Forrest Pogue, Interview with George C. Marshall, tape 19, recorded on 20 November 1956, 562. http://www.marshallfoundation.org/library/pogue.html (accessed 19 March 2014).

[10]Dean Acheson, *Present at the Creation, My Years in the State Department* (New York: W.W. Norton and Company, 1969), 371.

[11]See George F. Kennan, *Memoirs: 1925-1950* (Boston: Little, Brown and Co., 1967), 1: 315-345 for Kennan's perspective as Director for Policy Planning under George C. Marshall and Dean Acheson.

Kennan's understanding and expertise in Soviet political nuances. Kennan had also served as the first Deputy for Foreign Affairs of the newly formed National War College in 1946.[12]

There was one other Soviet specialist in the State Department who was considered to be of "par excellence" with Mr. Kennan. The second Department of State Soviet specialist was Chip Bohlen. Chip Bohlen served as a State Department Councilor to the Secretary of State. Bohlen served the Secretary of State from August, 1947 to August, 1949. Together these two State Department experts on the Soviet government were the primary engines of the Policy Planning Staff. Kennan and Bohlen developed and shaped U.S. policy towards the Soviet Union. Their knowledge and style directly impacted the development and articulation of policy during the early post World War II years.

The Policy Planning Staff reflected the leadership style of the Director. George Kennan ran the Policy Planning Staff as a highly personalized operation.[13] Kennan gathered input from his planning staff until he determined that he had sufficient data and analysis. Kennan would then point retreat to an office in the Library of Congress where he could think and write without interruption. Kennan would write and craft his report and continue to polish the product alone. Nitze characterized the end result as a "superbly written report." When Kennan finished he would consider the final product as "etched in steel."[14] The policy papers would be then be forwarded to the Department of State for further analysis, discussion and ultimately policy approval or disapproval.

The Policy Planning Staff shifted styles and leadership under the direction of Paul Henry Nitze. Paul H. Nitze joined the Policy Planning Staff in the summer of 1949. Nitze served as a

---

[12]Institute for Advanced Studies, http://www.ias.edu/people/kennan (accessed 20 March 2014).

[13]Paul H. Nitze, *From Hiroshima to Glasnost, At the Center of Decision, A Memoir* (New York: Grove Weidenfeld, 1989), 85.

[14]Ibid.

Deputy Director for George Kennan. Nitze assumed duties as the Policy Planning Staff Director on January 1st of 1950. George Kennan left the State Department and would serve as Ambassador to the Soviet Union in 1952 and later, as Ambassador to Yugoslavia from 1960 to 1963. Paul Nitze's previous governmental experiences included procurement of strategic commodities abroad. The experience influenced how he conducted business as the Director of the PPS. Nitze came to recognize that the work load was simply too great for one individual to manage. "I had learned that it was often necessary to delegate responsibility to others, even though I often believed that the results could have been better had I done the work myself. Most of the time, of course, I was wrong; the procurement business during the war was so vast and complex that it was simply beyond the capabilities of one person to manage all of it."[15] This realization shaped Nitze in the construction of policy. Nitze would ultimately become responsible for the creation of NSC 68. His recommendations as part of NSC 68 set in motion a significant policy shift towards the Soviet Union. His experiences and leadership style would shape how NSC 68 came into existence.

Nitze considered the Policy Planning Staff as a collaborative and group effort. Policy Planning Staff member Dorothy Fosdik stated "Paul was more interested in a consensus view" and that "he didn't think he had the answers, he felt that he had to use the wisest brains." Typically one staff member would write the first draft followed by a separate staff member creating a second draft and so forth. Robert Tufts noted "Mr. Nitze didn't like to write and didn't write except when he had to." So rather than Nitze handing down finished products like George F. Kennan did, "I [Tufts] and other members of the staff would produce papers which he [Nitze] then criticized."[16] Nitze would ultimately assume responsibility for the draft once be believed that

---

[15]Ibid., 86.

[16]David Callahan, *Dangerous Capabilities, Paul Nitze and the Cold War* (New York: Harper Collins Publishers, 1990), 96.

sufficient analysis of complex issues had been clarified. Nitze decided the "staff's position and for the wording of the final report, even if a majority, or all, of the other members were against me."[17]

Differences of style for creating policy would leave Nitze's "finger prints" as the author of the recommended policy, NSC 68. Policy Planning Staff members noted that Kennan's style was a brilliance and eloquence in outlining containment. PPS members stated that Nitze's style had a forcefulness of argument and command of facts. The forceful argument of NSC 68 would be a signature trademark of Nitze as compared to a compelling articulate argument under Kennan's style. "He [Nitze] wasn't very articulate compared to George Kennan," said Carlton Savage, "but he was more concise."[18] Paul Nitze's style and his management of staff actions would be fully displayed in NSC 68. Similarly, analysis and critiques of NSC 68 reflected on Nitze's influence and commentary on the document. Nitze shaped these critiques during the State-Defense Policy Working Groups with external experts analyzing NSC 68 recommendations. These working groups were detailed discussions of why the recommendations were suggested. The working groups provided additional insight into the mind of Nitze and the collective thoughts of the PPS working group.

Atomic Bomb Experiences & Other Influences

Paul Nitze had previously been a member of the United States Strategic Bombing Survey (USSBS). The experience would shape Nitze's thoughts about capabilities and limitations of nuclear weapons. The strategic survey gave Nitze an opportunity to see firsthand the effects of bombings, fire raids and the devastation of the atomic bombs at Nagasaki and Hiroshima. Nitze and the USSBS interviewed people as well as physically walked the ground where the atomic

---

[17]Nitze, 86.
[18]Callahan, 97.

bombs had detonated. He observed the effects of radiation and the intense heat from the atomic

bomb detonations, remarking:

> In one firebomb raid against Tokyo in March 1945 the AAF (Army Air Forces) inflicted casualties of 83,600 killed and destroyed nearly 16 square miles of the city. The significance of the atomic bomb was that it compressed the explosive power of many conventional bombs into one and thus enormously enhanced the effectiveness of a single bomber. With each plane carrying ten tons of high explosives and incendiaries, the attacking force required to equal the effects of a single atomic weapon would have been 210 B-29s at Hiroshima and 120 B-29s at Nagasaki.[19]

Nitze noted the effects of the bomb were initially devastating. If the population had sufficient

warning and protection from the initial blast and radiation the effects could be mitigated. Nitze

saw that nuclear weapons were survivable, "he carried away the lesson that nuclear weapons did

not necessarily mean no victor or loser in a future war. He also came away convinced of the

importance of always being prepared for the worst."[20]

The development and influence of NSC 68 began with the detection of airborne

radioactive dust particles. This collection of radioactive dust signified the loss of a monopoly on

the atomic bomb. The Air Force's Long Range Detection System detected a significant amount of

radioactive particles on September 3, 1949. The dust particles were collected downwind from a

suspected Soviet test range by an Air Force WB-29 reconnaissance aircraft stationed in Alaska.[21]

The Soviets successfully tested a nuclear weapon sometime between 3 September and a week

prior. Soviet capabilities continued to expand. The collection of radioactive dust particles

conveyed the strategic message that the United States had lost the monopoly on atomic

knowledge. President Truman announced to U.S. citizens and the free world the successful

nuclear test by Soviet Union on 23 September 1949. The announcement had a particular

---

[19]Nitze, 43.

[20]May, 4.

[21]Nitze, 82.

psychological effect on the U.S. Government and citizens alike. The successful Soviet nuclear

detonation was several years ahead of projected dates.[22]

The year 1949 ended with a sour note for the Truman administration. The successful

nuclear detonation by the Soviet Union with the developing Chinese situation had a psychological

impact on the U.S. government. The Chinese Communists were gaining momentum over the

Chinese Nationalist Party. The Chinese Communist Party consolidated power after the struggle

with the Chinese Nationalist Chiang Kai-shek. The Chinese Nationalists fled to Taiwan. Mao

Tse-Tsung and Communist China signed a treaty with the Soviet Union on 14 February 1950.

The strengthening bonds between the two communist countries intensified concern between the

Department of State and the Department of Defense about communist policy unity. According to

Nitze the State Department was not by surprised. The successful Soviet nuclear detonation and

the Chinese National Party departure from mainland China occurred in a very short period. The

occurrence of these activities within a small window of time garnered additional attention within

Department of State and Department of Defense. There was a perception that there could

potentially be a fundamental shift of the established balance of power.[23]

The successful Soviet detonation created an additional dimension to nuclear weapons

discussions, analysis and U.S. nuclear policy. The U.S. government was debating whether to

press forward with research and development of a thermonuclear weapon utilizing the concept of

nuclear fusion. President Truman would ask if the Russians could build a thermonuclear weapon.

The successful "Soviet achievement did do was to pose the choices now available to the United

States in stark terms: should it move away from reliance on atomic weapons toward a greater

emphasis on conventional warfare capabilities, or should it build more such devices – in an effort

---

[22]Drew, 17.

[23]Nitze, 87.

to maintain indefinite nuclear superiority over the Russians?"[24] Successful Soviet achievement in the nuclear field reinforced the argument for conventional forces. Nitze used the argument of eventual Soviet nuclear parity to justify enhancing conventional force capabilities. Capable and well-trained conventional forces combined with modern state of the art weaponry would serve to deter overly ambitious Soviet aggression.

George Kennan elaborated upon the impact of the successful Soviet nuclear detonation. The Soviet Union at the time of their successful test detonation in August of 1949 did not possess more than a couple of nuclear bombs. The Soviets would refine the technical aspects required for constructing nuclear bombs over a relatively finite period of time. The Soviets would transition to building a significant inventory of nuclear bombs when they improved their technical capabilities. The question would transition to how many bombs could they produce in the short time and what quantity of weapons would they possess within three to five years? A nuclear weapons stalemate could result in a limited nuclear exchange. The limited nuclear exchange would transitioned to a predominantly conventional fight. A nuclear weapons stalemate could also prevent a nuclear exchange and lead directly to a purely conventional fight. The fact that the Soviet Union now had successfully detonated a nuclear bomb, he suggested, at a future point in time might well make it "impossible for us to retaliate with the atomic bomb [even] against a Russian attack with orthodox weapons."[25] The new Soviet capability could lend itself towards justifying sustainment or expansion of a conventional military capability. The potential for a purely conventional conflict with an aggressive Soviet or communist foe would justify Nitze's forceful argument in NSC 68 for increasing expenditures. The potential for a future conventional conflict would

---

[24]John Lewis Gaddis, *The Long Peace, Inquiries Into the History of the Cold War* (New York: Oxford University Press, 1987), 112.

[25]George Kennan speech to the National Defense Committee of the Chamber of Commerce of the United States, January 23, 1947, enclosed in Kennan to Dean Acheson, August 21, 1950, "Memoranda of Conversations, August, 1950," Dean Acheson Papers, Box 65, Harry S. Truman Library. See also George F. Kennan, *Memoirs: 1925-1950,* (Boston: Little, Brown and Company, 1967), 1: 310-12.

support expanding capabilities of conventional U.S. forces. Additionally, it would support sustaining future expenses associated with growing conventional force capabilities. Furthermore, "the significance was that Soviet atomic capabilities might neutralize the diplomatic shadows heretofore cast by the U.S. atomic monopoly. Enemies and allies would both doubt U.S. willingness to risk nuclear war over limited issues; hence the United States would no longer have the means to encourage allies or intimidate foes."[26]

President Harry S. Truman approved further research and development of the thermonuclear bomb. The President and the Special Committee discussed the issue on 31 January 1950. President Truman asked, "Can the Russians do it [develop the thermonuclear bomb]?" Some believe his mind was already decided. The meeting did not last beyond ten minutes.[27] In the same action he signed a letter directing "the Secretary of State and the Secretary of Defense to undertake a reexamination of our objectives in peace and war and of the effect of these objectives on our strategic plans, in the light of the probable fission bomb capability and possible thermonuclear bomb capability of the Soviet Union."[28] The president authorized the analysis which would lead to NSC 68.

Two unique political events were almost simultaneously unfolding during this period. The events may have added further impetus for a national security policy review. The political environment was highly sensitive and charged when discussing communism inside of the U.S. government and the actions of a communist Kremlin. The Alger Hiss case was in court. The Hiss case was a public trial for the American public to observe. Alger Hiss was a U.S. State Department employee on trial for charges of being a Soviet spy. The first case against Hiss ended

---

[26]Melvyn P. Leffler, *A Preponderance of Power: National Security, The Truman Administration, and the Cold War* (Stanford: Stanford University Press, 1992), 357.

[27]Nitze, 91.

[28]*Foreign Relations of the United States,* 1950, Vol. I, *National Security Affairs; Foreign Economic Policy,* 142.

in a hung jury in July 1949. A second trial was initiated against him in November of 1949.[29] Hiss was convicted of perjury on January 22, 1950 for lying about providing government secrets to Whittaker Chambers, a self-confessed Soviet agent handler.[30] The Alger Hiss case increased public concern about communism.

A similar event to the Alger Hiss case was occurring overseas with American allies. The United Kingdom was trying Klaus Fuchs. Klaus Fuchs was a German-born theoretical physicist. Fuchs concentrated in quantum physics at the University of Bristol. Fuchs served as the Chief of Theoretical Physics Division of British Atomic Energy Research.[31] Fuchs and a select group of British scientists had worked with the U.S. Army as part of the Manhattan Project. He was responsible for many of the significant theoretical calculations relating to the first nuclear weapons and early versions of the hydrogen bomb. Fuchs admitted to passing information to the Soviets on January 13, 1950. Fuchs was tried on March 1, 1950. He was charged that "at least four times between 1943 and 1947 that he had communicated to a person unknown information relating to atomic research which was calculated to be, or might be directly or indirectly, useful to an enemy."[32] The trial was only an hour and a half long and Fuchs admitted that he was guilty. His arrest and potential espionage of nuclear secrets for the Soviet Union raised fears of the U.S.S.R. closing the technology gap between the West and the United States. The other fear to gain traction was that if the Soviets could penetrate U.S. and allied nuclear weapons research and development, what other secret operations were the Soviets accessing?

---

[29]Susan Jacoby, *Alger Hiss and the Battle for History* (New Haven: Yale University Press, 2009), 7.

[30]John Earl Haynes, Harvey Klehr, and Alexander Vassiliev, *Spies: The Rise and Fall of the KGB in America* (New Haven: Yale University Press, 2009), 2.

[31]Allen M. Hornblum, *The Invisible Harry Gold, The Man Who Gave the Soviets the Atomic Bomb* (New Haven: Yale University Press, 2009), 119.

[32]Robert C. Williams, *Klaus Fuchs, Atom Spy* (Cambridge, MA: Harvard University Press, 1987), 126–131.

Threat Analysis and Policy Report

The ensuing report developed was deliberately broad in scope. The report was expansive in nature because of the complexity of the problems associated with a tasking. The report may have been even broader in nature than President Truman anticipated. Steven Reardon argued that the broad and sweeping language of NSC 68 "would serve as the basic guide for similar papers generated over the next decade."[33] Nitze states the approach of NSC 68 served as an example for other policy papers. The NSC 68 example may have been the greatest contribution as Nitze elaborated, "The papers up to that date dealt largely with the major components of policy rather than policy as a whole...I think the important thing about the paper was the comprehensiveness of the approach rather that then particular recommendations contained therein."[34] If the policy approach or intent was to address an over-arching comprehensiveness, then the policy recommendations could be rather generalized. The generalizations could be suspect because of the very lack of detailed analysis or thoroughness. The recommendation would be put together for review by President Truman. Initially the president would not sign the recommended policy. President Truman referred the paper for further analysis and discussion by the National Security Council.

The development of the draft policy paper which would become NSC 68 was done in relatively short order. Department of State staff along with Department of Defense staff coordinated sufficiently. Indications were that neither agency had a self-serving agenda or an organizational interest to undermine or subvert the report. Department of State Policy Planning

---

[33]Steven L. Rearden, *The Evolution of American Strategic Doctrine, Paul H. Nitze and the Soviet Challenge* (Richmond, VA: Johns Hopkins Foreign Policy Institute, School of Advanced International Studies, 1984), 19.

[34]Testimony of Paul H. Nitze, June 17, 1960, in U.S. Congress, Senate Committee on Government Operations, Subcommittee on National Policy Machinery, *Hearings: Organizing for National Security: The Department of State, The Policy Planning Staff, and the National Security Council*, 86 Cong., 2d sess., Washington, DC: U.S. Government Printing Office, 1960, 879.

Staff consisted of a total of nine members, including Paul Nitze. Department of Defense planners included Major General (MG) James H. Burns who served as Secretary of Defense Louis Johnson's deputy for politico-military affairs. MG Burns served as the Secretary of Defense's Liaison Officer (LNO) with the State department.[35] MG Burns' health was not the best and he frequently only worked approximately half a day during the development of NSC 68.[36] Nitze requested support from the Joint Chiefs of Staff in order to have direct access to the Joint Chiefs of Staff during the planning. Major General Truman "Ted" Landon was appointed. MG Landon served as the Air Force representative to the Joint Strategic Survey Committee. He provided additional expertise to the task at hand, "I found him to be a wise, straightforward, and competent collaborator."[37]

NSC 68 was initiated at the end of January. The policy analysis gained momentum in February of 1950. Major General Landon initially did not offer substantive comment on current issues. According to Nitze, MG Landon was eventually persuaded that the State Department group was "serious about doing a basic strategic review and not just writing some papers which would help people promote special projects of one kind or another." Nitze realized that MG Landon's evolving perception of the project was a "revolt from within" the Pentagon as it pertained to the policies of the Secretary of Defense, Louis Johnson.[38] The policy analysis turned the corner by conducting a strategic analysis and review. NSC 68 was a major milestone given the fact that Secretary of Defense Louis Johnson and the Joint Staff were attempting to control Department of Defense expenditures. The post-war budgets reflected relatively tight fiscal constraints. The leadership desired to return to a balanced budget after supporting World War II.

---

[35]Acheson, 371.

[36]Nitze, 93.

[37]Ibid.

[38]Rearden, 19.

The fiscal policy of restraint also emanated from a strong constituent current demanding that the government reign in the national budget to achieve a balanced budget. Louis Johnson wanted limited military expenditures, "the Secretary of Defense (SecDef) was committed to a defense budget on no more than $13.5 billion, and the President himself had earlier gone on record as favoring cutting the existing defense budget to between $5 and $7 billion."[39] The President's initial spending plan for the year was for spending levels not to exceed $13 billion to cover expenses for the Army, Navy and Air Force. The projected spending plan did not quite amount to one-third of the federal budget projection. The projected spending amounted to just under five percent of gross national product.[40]

The staffing of NSC 68 included input and analysis from multiple external consultants. Paul Nitze and the Policy Planning Staff requested external analysis four different times with experts to provide additional feedback. The discussions between the State-Defense Policy Working Group and the external consultants contained multiple themes that were discussed by all of the consultants. A distinct concern was articulated about the public understanding of the Soviet threat. If the public was properly informed and kept aware of governments actions then the public support necessary to execute such a strategy could be successful. The consultants verbalized the concern of the introduction of a "garrison state." They were very concerned about the loss of the very freedoms they were seeking to protect. Citizens must be informed about the importance of what their government was doing to protect them from the Soviets. The U.S. government would lose legitimacy and the support of its citizens if the government over-stepped its boundaries to encroach or endanger those very freedoms. Multiple consultants also engaged the group about long-term engagement with the Soviets. The consultants asked about the ability to live with,

---

[39]Harry S. Truman, White House news conference, 16 October 1948, *The New York Times* (17 October 1948).

[40]May, preface vii.

19

negotiate or simply to tolerate the Soviets. The consultants believed that over the long-term the Soviet system would be subject to decay and internal dissent. A final consistent theme was that the analysis may have under estimated the potential economic power and moral strength of the United States and the free world. The consultants believed that there was an undeniable strength or power that was present but not fully accounted for in the analysis.

The PPS met as part of the State-Defense Policy Review Group on Monday, 27 February 1950 with Dr. Oppenheimer, who was serving at Princeton University.[41] Discussion between the State-Defense Policy Review Group and Dr. Oppenheimer dealt with the morality of the atomic bomb, the employment of this devastating weapon and the relationship of the atomic weapon regarding military and economic strength. Dr. Oppenheimer wondered if the paper would present a recognizable picture to the average citizen of the Soviet Union. Dr. Oppenheimer asked if we were so sure that the comparison was one between jet black and pure white. Mr. Nitze said that he did not think that we had given that impression.[42] Dr. Oppenheimer's discussion asked if the State-Defense Working group tone was too strident. Dr. Oppenheimer supported the paper's argument for hope and freedom when he stated, "first this is to stand as an example which will inspire those who are drifting toward a concept of neutrality. We must give back to France the hope they gave to us and the rest of the world in the age of enlightenment."[43]

The second State-Defense Policy Review group met Thursday, March 2, 1950 with Dr. James B. Conant. Dr. Conant was President of Harvard University and a member of the General

---

[41]*Foreign Relations of the United States,* 1950, Vol. I, *National Security Affairs; Foreign Economic Policy*, 168-69. Dr. Oppenheimer at this time was Chairman of the Institute for Advanced Study located at Princeton but a separate entity from Princeton; concurrently the Chairman of the Advisory Committee of the United States Atomic Energy Commission; Director of Los Alamos Laboratories of Manhattan Engineer District, 1943-1945.

[42]Ibid., 171.

[43]Ibid.

Advisory Committee of the United States Atomic Energy Commission.[44] Dr. Conant's discourse with the review group articulated similar concerns as the discussion with Dr. Oppenheimer. One concern of Dr. Conant's was the fear of winning the war against the Soviets and securing Europe while losing that which we cherished most, the loss of our freedoms.[45] Dr. Conant discussed the policy analysis of the Soviet Union with long-term goals of Soviet decline and decay. He predicted the ruin of the Soviets in economic, social and moral terms, thus potentially reinforcing one of the recommended policy themes of maximizing economic strength and competition against the Soviets. Dr. Conant argued "that by 1980 their absurdities and static system would cause them to grind to a stop...the competition between our dynamic free society and static slave society should be all in our favor, or if not, then we deserve to lose."[46]

The third meeting consisted of two advisory consultants; Mr. Chester I. Barnard and Dr. Henry D. Smyth. The two advisors met with the State-Defense Policy Review Group on Friday, March 10, 1950.[47] Mr. Barnard and Dr. Smyth were in relative agreement with the recommendations. Dr. Smyth's final comment was particularly insightful towards the emotional and logical generalizations Nitze and the PPS developed in NSC 68. Dr. Smyth stated, "the one thing he missed in the paper was a gospel which lends itself to preaching." Mr. Nitze said, "that that something we had in mind and it might be more appropriate in the form of a speech written for the President than as an integral part of the study."[48]

---

[44]Ibid., 176.

[45]Ibid.

[46]Ibid., 179.

[47]Ibid., 190. Mr. Chester I. Barnard was the President of the Rockefeller Foundation; Member of the Board of Consultants of the Secretary of State's Committee on Atomic Energy, 1946. Dr. Henry D. Smyth was serving as a current Member of the Atomic Energy Commission.

[48]*Foreign Relations of the United States, 1950,* Vol. I, *National Security Affairs; Foreign Economic Policy,* 195.

The fourth consultant to meet with the State-Defense Policy Review Group was an economic/business oriented individual, Robert A. Lovett. Mr. Lovett met with the review group on Thursday, March 16, 1950.[49] He approached the proposed paper from an economic standpoint with banking experience and working in the Pentagon for the Army during World War II. Mr. Lovett agreed with much of the paper and commented that one of the challenges would be to inform and "give the facts" to the American people. In the Conclusion he recommended, "that the Conclusions should be stated simply and clearly, and in almost telegraphic style, or in what he referred to as 'Hemmingway sentences.'"[50] Mr. Lovett's recommendation included addressing the communist threat "in the field of ideas and this means we must capitalize on our standard of living, the role of the individual, and the fact that our system is based on a freedom of choice."[51] He encouraged the idea that the U.S. aggressively engage the Soviet Union from an economic perspective and "we make a thorough study of all economic warfare possibilities, including preemptive buying."[52]

Dr. Ernest O. Lawrence was the final consultant engaged by the State-Defense Policy Review Group. The meeting occurred on Monday, March 20th of 1950.[53] Dr. Lawrence's discussion focused on two aspects. The first was on continuing scientific research and the second emphasis was on scientists' positive energy associated with the ability to use "magnificent facilities" to further their scientific investigation and research into atomic energy and weapons.[54]

---

[49]Ibid., 196. Mr. Robert A. Lovett was a banker; he served as Assistant Secretary of War for Air, April 1941-November 1945; the Under Secretary of State, July 1947-January, 1949; appointed Deputy Secretary of Defense, September 1950.

[50]Ibid., 197-98.

[51]Ibid., 198.

[52]Ibid.

[53]Ibid., 200. Dr. Ernest O. Lawrence was a nuclear physicist who was Director of the Radiation Laboratory, University of California; inventor of the cyclotron; participant in the atomic bomb development program during the Second World War.

[54]Ibid., 201.

He amplified the positivity associated with scientific research in that scientific research continued to expand the number and quality of physicists. Dr. Lawrence's "Major thesis was that our safety lies in being farther ahead scientifically and productively than the Russians."[55]

The State-Defense Policy Review Group meetings with external consultants served as a positive experience for the Review Group to solidify their assessments and recommendations. There was a significant amount of agreement in support of the paper from all of the consultants, however there were points of contention as well. Overall, the consultants consistently talked about the importance and necessity of public awareness. Public support would be critical for understanding and addressing the context of the Soviet threat. Public support would be decisive for increasing budgetary expenditures. Long-term execution of a comprehensive strategy would require an indefatigable well of public support. The discussion with the consultants reinforced the group's belief that firmly but patiently engaging the Soviets politically, economically, and militarily could shape their behavior and actions.

The policy analysis addressed the concern of balancing collective security and freedom. The report forcefully argued that it was the freedom of the individual from an overbearing, coercive or even tyrannical government that provided a moral strength and edge. The aggressive communist policies were oppressive to their own people. Eventually the people under the communist collective would not tolerate any more oppression. The great strength of the West and the United States was derived from moral legitimacy.

The consultants discussed the potential benefits of negotiations with the working group. The potential benefits of negotiations over a long term would provide access into the Soviet system. Long term negotiations would additionally offer opportunity to explore weaknesses in the Soviet system. The potential of negotiations reinforced the argument of dealing with the

---

[55]Ibid., 201.

communism from a high moral view point. The analysis applied the legitimacy of the free citizens being consensually governed versus the Soviet "slavery" to argue for an increase of conventional military and economic capability.

Finally, the economic strength of the U.S. and the free world was reinforced as a critical component. The economy and the underlying economic potential of the free world remained to be developed. The economic capability was viewed as a critical lever to bring about change within the Soviet system. The policy analysis argued that the U.S. economy could easily absorb any recommendations presented without serious repercussions to the global economy. Soviet economic capability could not match the economic potential of the free world.

The consultant suggestions and critiques reinforced State-Defense Policy Review Group member positions. The suggestions and concerns were integrated into the policy analysis. The recommendations solidified refinement of the final product. The policy analysis and recommendations supported the arguments. The State-Defense Policy Review Group recommended forwarding the proposed policy to President, Harry S. Truman.

NSC 68's introduction described the significant conflicts which led to the current environment. Chapter II described The Fundamental Purpose of the United States. Chapter II was juxtaposed in Chapter III, The Fundamental Design of the Kremlin. NSC 68 then described the conflict of Ideas and Values between the U.S. Purpose and the Kremlin Design in Chapter IV. The next two chapters analyzed Soviet and U.S. Intentions and Capabilities (Actual and Potential). Chapter VII articulated the Present Risks. Chapter VIII discussed Atomic Weapons from U.S. and U.S.S.R. capabilities, Stockpiling and Use of Atomic Weapons and concludes with discourse of the International Control of Atomic Energy. NSC 68 mentioned four courses of action (COA): Continuation of Current Policies, Isolation, War and finally, a Rapid Build-up of Political, Economic, and Military Strength in the Free World. NSC 68 closed with a Conclusion chapter and a Recommendation chapter. The Recommendation urged the adoption of the fourth course of action; a Rapid Build-up of Political, Economic, and Military Strength in the Free World.[56]

The first course of action, a Continuation of Current Policies served as a policy of "no change." The course of action could be considered a straw-man or throw away course of action. The COA did not address changing the issues confronting the U.S. and its policies towards communism. Sustained political, economic, military and diplomatic actions under the current course of action would not enhance power, capability or prestige of the west and the United States. The course of action noted that the "United States has a large potential military capability but an actual capability which, though improving, is declining relative to the U.S.S.R." Economically the current policies "will not produce a solution to the problem of international economic equilibrium…and will not create an economic base conducive to political stability in many important free countries." The United States and other free countries would only sustain the current posture under this course of action. Ultimately the capabilities and potential of the U.S. would shift to a defensive posture while the Soviet system progressively expanded. This course of action did not enable the U.S. and the free world to challenge or limit Soviet expansionism. The United States would not be able to influence or limit Soviet actions and "will not be successful in checking and rolling back the Kremlin's drive.[57]

The second course of action, Isolationism was even less appealing in the analysis. Isolationism would result in the withdrawal of the United States from the free world. U.S. isolationism would not check Soviet political, economic and military designs. The significant argument against isolationism as a course of action remained that the "Soviets Union would quickly dominate most of Eurasia." The Soviets would maximize capabilities of the Eurasian land

---

[56]*Foreign Relations of the United States,* 1950, Vol. I, *National Security Affairs; Foreign Economic Policy*, 235-292.

[57]Ibid., 276-279.

25

mass. The capabilities and potential of the Eurasian land mass would represent "a potential far superior to our own, and would promptly proceed to develop this potential with the purpose of eliminating our power." The undeveloped potential exceeded the capabilities and potential of the United States and Western Europe combined. The Soviets could simply intimidate Western Europe and dominate all free countries without fear of the United States. Ultimately, "isolation would in the end condemn us to capitulate or to fight alone and on the defensive." This course of action was unacceptable since it argued that "there would be no negotiation, unless on the Kremlin's terms, for we would have given up everything of importance."[58]

War as the third course of action was "generally unacceptable to Americans." There was a population of Americans who favored deliberate action against the Soviets in the near future. The belief that an offensively decisive blow could delivered with sufficiency to prevent the Soviets from retaliating was not possible. A preventative war was seen as likely become a drawn out conflict since "the operations alone would not force or induce the Kremlin to capitulate." The offensive action would be viewed as morally corrupt, "repugnant to many Americans" and not considered a "just war."[59] The offensive assault would provide the Kremlin the legitimate manifestation of the argument that it was the free world who was aggressive, domineering and sought control over the world. This course of action could be seen as a throw-away course of action. Historically as a rule of thumb, the United States did not support aggressive and offensive conflict with other governments or systems. This COA was politically untenable.

The fourth and final course of action was a "Rapid Build-up of Political, Economic, and Military Strength in the Free World." This course of action recommended an increased rate for building the political, economic and military strength. The analysis argued that the fourth course

---

[58]Ibid., 279-280.
[59]Ibid., 281-282.

of action was the only means "consistent with the progress toward achieving our fundamental purpose." Military capability should be expanded in order to meet and deter any potential Soviet military threat while being able "to support our foreign policy." Expanded political and economic power would "reduce the influence of the Kremlin inside the Soviet Union and other areas under its control." The political and economic growth would help "win the peace and frustrate the Kremlin design." Economic analysis supported this course of action. The economy could be sustained over a long period of time without a "real decrease in the standard of living." This course of action through rapid political, economic and military growth would also provide a "psychological" advantage missing in the other COAs. The rapid build-up would provide a "revival of confidence and hope in the future."[60]

NSC 68 as written analysis is general in nature and vague with regards to specific details for much of the document. The fourth course of action was the longest and described in the greatest detail. The last COA provided greater economic analysis when compared to the other three courses of action. The manner in which the courses of action were written lends support to the argument that the report describes the Communist bloc as "monolithic and evil in nature."[61] The report does not analyze or account for political, military and economic differences inherent in the greater Union of Soviet Socialist Republics. Nitze states that he left out certain economic details in the report in order to facilitate approval of the recommendations. The report contained no financial figures. Nitze told Secretary Acheson what he believed the estimates would be. Acheson responded, "don't put any such figure into this report. It is right for you to estimate it and tell me about it and I will tell Mr. Truman, but the decision on the amount of money to be

[60]Ibid., 282-287.

[61]Samuel F. Wells, Jr., "Sounding the Tocsin: NSC 68 and the Soviet Threat," *International Security* (Fall 1979): 139.

requested of the Congress should not be made until it has been costed out in detail. One first ought to decide whether this is the kind of policy one wants to follow."[62]

The report was initially submitted to the National Security Council for the President Truman's review on April 7, 1950. President Truman returned the report to the National Security Council for additional analysis and discussion. The initial report submitted to President Truman deliberately left out some major details. President Truman focused on what specific programs were recommended. The president requested additional details about projected costs associated with the recommended programs, "He [President Truman] requested that the NSC give a clear indication of programs envisaged in the Report, including estimates of their probable cost."[63] NSC 68 would undergo multiple iterations after the initial submission to President Truman on 14 April 1950. President Truman's premise of maintaining fiscal responsibility would be given additional support for an increase in military expenditure when North Korea attacked on South Korea in the summer of 1950. NSC 68 would undergo additional analysis with other actions through four more reviews with President Truman. President Truman met with his National Security Council on 14 December of 1950 "to consider the revised proposals for implementing the strategy as contained in NSC 68/3." With only minor modifications, those proposals were "approved as a working guide for the urgent purpose of making an immediate start" in NSC 68/4, issued later that same day.[64] President Truman issued a proclamation through a television and radio address on 16 December 1950 when NSC 68/4 was approved and initially implemented.

NSC 68 recommendations impacted the budget. The 1951 basic defense bill was $13.3 billion dollars. Congress supported and passed two defense supplementals totaling $35.3 billion

---

[62]Nitze, 97.

[63]*Foreign Relations of the United States,* 1950, Vol. I, *National Security Affairs; Foreign Economic Policy*, 293-294.

[64]Drew, 120.

dollars. President Truman submitted the first request July 19, 1950 and the second on December 1, 1950. The first supplemental request devoted the majority of funds towards build-up of capability and did not request a significant portion to support the initiation of hostilities on the Korean peninsula. The Chinese counterattack against United Nations forces prompted the President to ask for an immediate supplemental appropriation of $16.8 billion dollars for the Department of Defense.[65] This supplemental request was prior to the final revision of NSC 68. The defense budget and international affairs expenditures increased over 300% between fiscal year 1950 and 1953. The 1950 defense expenditure was $17.7 billion and reached $52.6 billion in 1953.[66]

NSC 68 served statesmen and policy makers as alarm warning of communist aggression. The American public was informed of an increasingly aggressive communist threat. The policy served as a first step toward addressing communist actions through a unified perspective. The recommendations enabled a reversal of historical post-war trends of reducing military capabilities and military spending. NSC 68 codified an overarching theme and began to address the Soviet threat but was formalized with only a few remaining years under Democratic leadership. What would follow NSC 68? Where would new Republican leadership take strategic policy? The answer was soon to arrive with the election of a Republican president, Dwight D. Eisenhower.

---

[65]Ibid., 112.
[66]Wells, 140.

PRESIDENT EISENHOWER, THE "NEW LOOK", PROJECT SOLARIUM AND NSC 162

President Eisenhower became the 34th President of the United States on Tuesday, the 20th

of January 1953. Eisenhower assumed the presidential office following Harry S. Truman. One of

President Eisenhower's election themes had been centered on U.S. national security and the

national security policy of his predecessor. President Dwight D. Eisenhower promised a "new

look" to address and review the strategic interests of the United States. Eisenhower further

campaigned on reviewing the U.S. national strategy. President Eisenhower had also campaigned

on his extensive military experience. Dwight D. Eisenhower's military background and fame

carried him to a substantial electoral victory while election campaigning. His experiences

managing large complex problems across significant organizations served him well. Eisenhower

worked with a lot of egotistical leaders and personalities, which also assisted him. Managing

complex problems and people would pay dividends during his presidential tenure. President

Eisenhower's "New Look" produced a new policy which would be known as NSC 162/2. NSC

162/2 was officially approved and signed by President Eisenhower on 30 October 1953.

President Eisenhower sought a compromise between national strategy and defense

balanced against a vigorous and robust economy. Dwight D. Eisenhower realized the current

spending increases that resulted from NSC 68 and NSC 135/3 would not be sustainable for an

indefinite period.[67] Journalists had commented on President Eisenhower's concern for balancing

the economic and military demands through what had been termed "the "Great Equation":

---

[67]NOTE: NSC 135 is a collection of eight reports by appropriate executive agencies. Overall, the report is approximately 500 pages total. NSC 135 recommendations are similar to those of NSC 68. NSC 135 recommends sustained diplomatic, economic and military containment with the U.S.S.R. and Soviet Satellites. NSC 135/3 recommends application of more resources to continental defense and civil defense programs in light of a nuclear attack. NSC 135/3 sought to address presidential question if additional resources were required immediately to redress an imbalance of requirements associated with atomic defense. Reference the Editorial Note, *Foreign Relations of the United States,* 1952-1954, Vol. II, *National Security Affairs*, 56 and 211.

balancing requisite military strength and healthy economic growth."[68] President Eisenhower's great equation roughly amounted to the following: security equaled spiritual force multiplied by economic force, multiplied by military force. If all of these elements were in proper balance then security should present. If one or more of these elements were near zero or at zero then the equation would amount to zero as well.[69]

The President sought a strategic security policy and military preparedness for a "long haul" that would ensure the security of the United States, Western Europe and the "free world" against the backdrop of a balanced budget and a strong U.S. economy.[70] President Eisenhower stated that "the great problem before his administration was to discover a reasonable and respectable posture of defense. If we can find such a level it may be possible to secure the money and resources necessary to enable the world to reach a decent economic position. In short, it may be possible to figure out a preparedness program that will give us a respectable position without bankrupting the nation."[71] The president recognized that security from a diplomatic, economic and military perspective had convinced him that "it is primarily our growing and combined strength that is bringing about a change in the Russian attitude."[72]

President Eisenhower's Background

President Eisenhower's military experiences influenced how he likely arrived at a point for determining a national strategy and a supporting strategic policy. Eisenhower's field-grade

---

[68]Charles J.V. Murphy, "The Eisenhower Shift: Part I," *Fortune* (January 1956): 87.

[69]Valerie L. Adams, *Eisenhower's Fine Group of Fellows: Crafting a National Security Policy to Uphold the Great Equation* (New York: Lexington Books, 2006), 2.

[70]Samuel P. Huntington, *The Common Defense* (New York: Columbia University Press, 1961), 67-68.

[71]*Foreign Relations of the United States, 1952-1954*, Vol. II, *National Security Affairs*, 236.

[72]Robert H. Bowie and Richard H. Immerman, *Waging Peace: How Eisenhower Shaped an Enduring Cold War Strategy* (New York: Oxford University Press, 1998), 118.

and senior military leader experiences influenced this thoughts and leadership about strategic policy. Eisenhower used those experiences to effectively shape the development and articulation of NSC 162/2. General Eisenhower was mentored early in his career by several significant military leaders of the period. Generals Fox Connor, John J. Pershing and Douglas MacArthur were some of the senior military leaders who had a formative impact on then Major Eisenhower's perception and understanding of military and political cultures. Eisenhower served three years under General Fox Connor as his chief of staff in Panama. General Connor continued to shape, develop and educate a young Eisenhower with military readings.[73] These leaders discussed strategy and tactics, successful and unsuccessful leaders, and at time the discussions even bordered on partisan politics. Eisenhower experienced one such period of blatant partisan politics in his formative years while he served as General MacArthur's chief aide, "beginning to verge on the political, even to the edge of partisan politics."[74] This experience shed light on what the potential future held for Eisenhower. The experience enlightened him with a broader appreciation and understanding of leadership in the context of a larger political and military environment.

President Eisenhower's military experiences combined with several key staff positions helped him formulate and hone his analytical skills, decision making and understanding of the strategy policy process. Eisenhower served as the War Department's Head for the War Plans Division under General George C. Marshall. He assumed duties as the Army Chief of Staff following General George C. Marshall in 1945. A significant event in General Eisenhower's military career was his involvement with the creation of the National Military Establishment as part of the National Security Act of 1947. One of Eisenhower's immediate actions was the development of a budget for the Department of the Army. The establishment of a service budget

---

[73]Grant W. Jones, "Education of the Supreme Commander: The Theoretical Underpinnings of Eisenhower's Strategy in Europe, 1944-45," *War and Society* 30, no. 2 (August 2011): 113.

[74]Dwight D. Eisenhower, *At Ease: Stories I Tell to Friends* (New York: Garden City, 1967), 213.

was a first as part of the 1947 National Security Act. General Eisenhower "put together the first integrated budget after unification (of the armed services under the National Military Establishment in 1947) for President Truman."[75] The experience of working budgetary issues enhanced his awareness and understanding of budgetary influences and how budgets could shape and influence national strategic policies.

The varied experiences of General Dwight D. Eisenhower influenced how he approached strategy. General Eisenhower commented during his tenure as the Chief of Staff of the Army that strategy must be much more encompassing. General Eisenhower felt that, "strategists must recognize that national security embraced a broad range of interests, especially a healthy economy."[76] His concern with strategy and the economy may have led to frustration serving under President Truman with the development and implementation of NSC 68 because he understood that the U.S. economy would shatter under the, "crushing weight of military power," strategists must recognize that "national security and national solvency are mutually dependent."[77]

General Eisenhower recognized other aspects of strategy must be carefully weighed in the development of a solid and effective strategic policy. Strategy and strategic policy should be complementary to each other. The strategic policy should be achieved while operating within the construct of the government, accepted societal norms and boundaries. The nations core values and democratic institutions could be placed in serious jeopardy if government was structurally altered. Altering norms by supporting an over-riding cause without respecting established checks

---

[75] William B. Pickett, *George F. Kennan and the Origins of Eisenhower's New Look, an Oral History of Project Solarium*, Princeton Institute for International and Regional Studies, Monograph Series, Number 1 (Princeton University, 2004), 38.

[76] Alfred D. Chandler Jr., and Louis Galamos Jr., *The Papers of Dwight D. Eisenhower* (Baltimore, MD, 1970), Vol. 11, 1312; Vol. 8, 1609.

[77] Ibid., Vol. 12, 659-660.

and balances creates a potential to usurp or centralize power within one or two branches of government. A strategic policy that could shift or pressure common values or institutions sufficiently enough to change common values or critical institutions was dangerous. The potential to change values or institutions into something no longer recognizable or respected by its citizens would not be acceptable or viable. The strategic policy would have to balance the values and systems that enabled America to be seen as a beacon of freedom to the rest of the world. Simultaneously the policy would have to address the challenges associated with managing communism. General Eisenhower articulated this in a letter when he stated, "The theory of defense against an aggressive threat must comprehend more than simple self-preservation; the security of spiritual and cultural values, including national and individual freedom, human rights, and the history of our nation and our civilization, are included."[78]

The New Look

President Eisenhower's inauguration address provided insight to the direction that the "new look" would take. The president stated that the United States should be guided by "fixed principles." Several principles listed below can be found in the arguments supporting or opposing a specific course of action. Key "principles" are listed below:

> The first principle includes, abhorring war as a chosen way to balk the purposes of those who threaten us, we hold it to be the first task of statesmanship to develop the strength that will deter the forces of aggression and promote the conditions of peace. In the light of this principle, we stand ready to engage with any and all others in joint effort to remove the causes of mutual fear and distrust among nations, so as to make possible drastic reduction of armaments. The sole requisites for undertaking such effort are that-- in their purpose--they be aimed logically and honestly toward secure peace for all.

> The president continued with the second principle, realizing that common sense and common decency alike dictate the futility of appeasement, we shall never try to placate an aggressor by the false and wicked bargain of trading honor for security. Americans, indeed, all free men, remember that in the final choice a soldier's pack is not so heavy a burden as a prisoner's chains.

---

[78]Ibid., Vol. 12, 488.

The third principle spoken by President Eisenhower, knowing that only a United States that is strong and immensely productive can help defend freedom in our world, we view our Nation's strength and security as a trust upon which rests the hope of free men everywhere. It is the firm duty of each of our free citizens and of every free citizen everywhere to place the cause of his country before the comfort, the convenience of himself.

President Eisenhower's sixth principle, recognizing economic health as an indispensable basis of military strength and the free world's peace, we shall strive to foster everywhere, and to practice ourselves, policies that encourage productivity and profitable trade. For the impoverishment of any single people in the world means danger to the well-being of all other peoples.[79]

President Eisenhower initiated a search for a strategy that incorporated the "long-haul" based on his experiences with other leaders and his positions of responsibility. President Eisenhower "supported the idea of a military buildup and increasing our strength in relationship to that of the Soviet Union, in the circumstance that had arisen, where the Soviet Union was still showing aggressive efforts. There was one thing in NSC 68 (although he, as I say, might not have identified it by number) that he did not accept, and as a matter of fact, I shared that view. NSC 68 as I remember it, postulated a date of maximum danger, and he didn't believe in that. The date was 1952, according to my recollection."[80] At that time and throughout his presidency, Eisenhower felt that we should organize and program for what he called the "long-pull" rather than working towards some arbitrary set date of maximum danger. He didn't see any evidence to support the idea that there was a date of maximum danger."[81]

The president was seeking an equitable medium, One of the things that does stand out – and is, in fact reproduced in NSC 162 – are the two facets of national security right from the very beginning. One is to meet the Soviet threat to U.S. security. The other is doing so without seriously weakening the U.S. economy or undermining our fundamental

---

[79]Dwight D. Eisenhower: "Inaugural Address," January 20, 1953. Online by Gerhard Peters and John T. Woolley, The American Presidency Project, http://www.presidency.ucsb.edu/ws/?pid=9600 (accessed 22 January 2014).

[80]Andrew J. Goodpaster, *Oral History Interview for the Dwight D. Eisenhower Library*, 1982, April 10, 2.

[81]Ibid.

values. And Eisenhower felt it absolutely essential to set a level of spending which you could maintain indefinitely without doing damage, as he saw it, to the economy.[82]

President Eisenhower's determination to provide a definitive and deliberate national strategy that balanced security, economic sustainability, and national values against a manipulative, coercive and subversive communist foe led to a staff exercise which would become known as the Solarium Project and lead ultimately to the strategic policy NSC 162.

Project Solarium

Project Solarium evolved from debate and decisions concerning the Department of Defense Budget for 1954. Discussions included commentary addressing what the overall policy objectives were. The special assistant directed a security policy analysis on 1 May 1953. Robert Cutler, the Special Assistant to the President for National Security Affairs to the Planning Board submitted 12 questions for further analysis for all the teams.[83] Cutler sought a paper that analyzed what current security policies existed. The NSC orchestrated President Truman's NSC papers 20/4, 68/2 and 135/3 along with President Eisenhower's NSC 153/1.

An off-record meeting initiated by President Dwight D. Eisenhower on 8 May 1953 set the stage for planning and execution of Project Solarium. The project was named after the solarium room on the top floor of the White House where it was conceived.[84] The meeting happened with Secretary of State John Dulles, CIA Director Allen W. Dulles, Secretary of the Treasury, George M. Humphrey, Under Secretary of State W.B. Smith, Special Assistant to the President, C.D. Jackson and Special Assistant to the President for National Security Affairs,

---

[82]Pickett, 39.

[83]See Appendix for all 12 Questions; reference *Foreign Relations of the United States,* 1952-54, Vol. II, *National Security Affairs,* 230-31.

[84]Pickett, 3.

Robert Cutler[85] in the White House Solarium.[86] The meeting topic centered on a general

discussion concerning the state of affairs between the East and the West and their relationship.

Secretary of State Dulles led part of the discussion concerning the state of affairs between the free

world and communism. He articulated three possible options for charting a change in strategic

policy based on what he perceived as a "fatal course for the free world" as directed under

President Truman. Dulles stated that unless "we change this policy, or get some break, we will

lose bit by bit the free world, and break ourselves financially."[87]

Secretary of State Dulles saw three different courses of action. The first possible course

of action would be the establishment of a "line and tell the Soviets that if one more country on

our side of the line should succumb to Communism by overt or covert aggression from the

outside or (more likely) cultivated indigenous uprising from within, that would be a casus belli

between the U.S. and the Soviets. This alternative risks global war."[88] The second potential

course of action proposed a limit line regarding Asia with a warning to Beijing and Moscow.

Dulles believed that this action "might not risk global war" and opined the establishment of an

Asian NATO.[89] He felt that this would be slow and time intensive. The third option centered on

---

[85]Walter Bedell Smith, referenced as W.B. Smith. *Foreign Relations of the United States,* 1952-1954, Vol. II, *National Security Affairs, Notes,* XXIV; General W.B. Smith, USA, Director of CIA until February 9, 1953; Under Secretary of State, February 9, 1953 – October 1, 1954. Charles Douglas Jackson, referenced as C.D. Jackson. *Foreign Relations of the United States,* 1952-1954, Vol. II, *National Security Affairs, Notes,* XX; Special Assistant to the President, February 16, 1953 – March 31, 1954; Member of the President's Committee on International Information Activities, 1953; Member of the U.S. Delegation to the Ninth Regular Session of the United Nations General Assembly, 1954. Expert on psychological warfare; served with OSS 1944 – 1945; Deputy Chief at Psychological Warfare Division, SHAEF. Robert Cutler, *Foreign Relations of the United States,* 1952-1954, Vol. II, *National Security Affairs, Notes,* XXVII; Administrative Assistant to the President, January 21, 1953 – March 22, 1953; thereafter Special Assistant to the President for National Security Affairs; Member of the President's Committee on International Information Activities, 1953.

[86]Robert Cutler, *No Time For Rest* (Boston: Little, Brown and Company, 1966), 307-309.

[87]Memorandum of conversation (assumed to be Cutler), May 8, 1953. Discussion derived from the memorandum.

[88]Bowie and Immerman, 124.

[89]Ibid.

an "attempt to restore the prestige of the West by winning in one or more areas a success or successes." Dulles felt the Communists continued to find success and the West in significant need of a victory, with "success for the free peoples is badly needed."[90] Conversation between Dulles and Eisenhower continued with Dulles recommendation for a policy that was considered "bold" with the goal of deterring further Communist advances and uplifting the spirit and morale of the West. Secretary Dulles also felt that a policy under this course of action could encourage liberty and democracy in the East. Such a course of action could also have significant implications to the Union of Soviet Socialist Republics in that it may cause the Soviets to think about their gains and to secure those advances prior to inclusion of any other countries.

The discussion generated further analysis by the president. President Eisenhower submitted that this conversation could be translated into an exercise for greater analysis of strategies to be applied when dealing with the U.S.S.R. Teams could be assembled with subject matter experts to conduct an in-depth and extremely thorough analysis of proposed options. President Eisenhower elaborated further, "when the teams are prepared, each should put on in some White House room, with maps, charts, all the basic supporting figures and estimates, just what each alternative would mean in terms of goal, risk, cost in money and men and world relations."[91]

Project Solarium was initiated and directed each team to exercise a directed but separate and distinct course of action. The three courses of action were to be analyzed in great detail as a way to identify if there existed a "best" possible future national security strategy. The process utilized is typically similar to the methodology utilized today. Today's methodology is known as the Military Decision Making Process or MDMP. This process is a very distinct and deliberate

---

[90]Ibid., 124.
[91]Ibid., 125.

manner in which the analysis is conducted. Typical planning process involves the creation of a

planning team that will generate multiple courses of action. The team will analyze each of the

courses of action. Distinct from this typical process is that each team had only one course of

action to analyze. Each team was directed to take possession of the directed course of action in

order to propose the benefits of the COA and defend the COA to the best of their ability.

The NSC received a brief from Robert Cutler on 13 May 1953. Project Solarium did not

begin in earnest for several more weeks due to exercise coordination and personnel staffing

requirements for the three teams. The Project Solarium exercise was executed utilizing the utmost

secrecy. Cutler, Smith and Allen Dulles supervised and facilitated the teams as well as established

a five man panel for determining the necessary guidance for each course of action. General James

Doolittle chaired the panel along with Robert Amory Jr.[92] Robert Amory Jr. served as the

Assistant Director of the Office of Research and Reports, in the Central Intelligence Agency

beginning March 17, 1953, finally becoming the Deputy for Intelligence in May of 1953.

Lieutenant General (LTG) Lyman L. Lemnitzer was a panel member who served as the Deputy

Chief of Staff for Plans and Research during the Project Solarium exercise and was "one of some

two-dozen persons picked personally by the president to make up the study's three task forces."[93]

Dean Rusk served as a Department of State political affairs expert as he recently departed the

---

[92]*Foreign Relations of the United States,* 1952-54, Vol. II, *National Security Affairs*, List of Persons, XV-XXVI; Amory, Robert, Jr., prior jobs include Acting Deputy Director for Intelligence from November 6, 1952; Assistant Deputy Director for Intelligence from February 19, 1953.

[93]Ibid., List of Persons, XXI; Lemnitzer, LTG Lyman L., USA (MG until August 1, 1952), served as Commander, 11th Airborne Division, 1950 and 7th Infantry Division, November, 1951; Deputy Chief of Staff for Plans and Research, United States Army, after August 1, 1952; Chief of Staff of the Army, July, 1957; Chairman of the Joint Chiefs of Staff, October 1, 1960 – September 30, 1962. See also, L. James Binder, *Lemnitzer, A Soldier for His Time* (Washington, DC: Brassey's, 1997), 197.

Department of State to lead the Rockefeller Foundation during the Solarium exercise.[94] The last

panel member was Admiral (ADM) Leslie C. Stevens who served as a Russian expert for the

panel. ADM Stevens had recently served three years as a naval attaché to the U.S. embassy in

Moscow.[95]

The panel posed factors consideration, "forces needed, cost in manpower, dollars,

casualties, world relations, intelligence estimates, time-tables, tactics in every other part of the

world while actions were being taken in a specific area, relations with the U.N. and Allies,

disposition of an area after gaining a victory therein, influencing world opinion and

Congressional action required."[96] The appointed board members were directed to meet in Room

376, Executive Offices Building, Washington, DC on Monday, 25 May 1953 to set the teams into

motion. The panel was expected to carry on until completion and to be finished no later than 1

June 1953. Solarium teams were expected to begin analysis in early June and finish within five to

six weeks at the latest.

Additionally the Solarium Exercise Panel directed four COAs to be excluded from the

three directed COAs as "being in conflict with the realities of the world situation."[97] The four

COAs determined for exclusion: "a drastic reduction of our armed strength and a determination

---

[94]*U.S. Department of State, Office of the Historian.* Rusk, David Dean, AB in Political Science, Davidson College, 1931. Rhodes Scholarship at St. John's College, Oxford University, B.S and M.A. degree. Served in the MI branch of the War Department, attained Deputy Chief of Staff in the Operations Division of the War Department's General Staff, discharged in 1946. Briefly served as assistant chief of the Division of International Security Affairs, Department of State's Office of Special Political Affairs before serving as special assistant to Secretary of War Robert Patterson. Served in several positions in Department of State from 1947 to 1951, including Director of the Office of Special Political Affairs, Assistant Secretary of State for International Organization Affairs, Deputy Under Secretary of State, and Assistant Secretary of State for East Asian and Pacific Affairs. Rusk headed the Rockefeller Foundation from 1952 to 1961. Rusk returned to the Department of State in January 1961 as President John F. Kennedy's Secretary of State. https://history.state.gov/departmenthistory/people/rusk-david-dean (accessed 5 February 2014).

[95]*New York Times*, Obituaries; Stevens, Leslie Clark, USN, naval attaché to the U.S. Embassy in Moscow, 1947 to 1950.

[96]Ibid., 323-28; Cutler Memorandum for Smith, May 15, 1953, lot 66D148, Secretary of State-National Security Council.

[97]*Foreign Relations of the United States,* 1952-54, Vol. II, *National Security Affairs*, 361-62.

not to fight except in the event of invasion of U.S. territory; rely solely upon the economic and military strength of the United States; a major change in the structure of international organization [Atlantic Union, World Government, etc.]; and contemplate the launching of a preventative war against the Soviet Union on our own initiative."[98]

Solarium Task Force Teams and Analysis Taskings

Appointed Task Force A members: Former Soviet Ambassador George F. Kennan [Chair] who had served as the Policy Planning Staff director prior to Paul H. Nitze and had recently served as an Ambassador to the Soviet Union.[99] Tyler C. Wood served as the Deputy to the Director, Mutual Security Agency (MSA) in 1953 and had previously served as the Deputy United States Special Representative in Europe in 1952.[100] Rear Admiral (RADM) H. Page Smith served as the Director of the Office of Foreign Military Affairs. RADM Smith was also a military planner and expert on Foreign Military Matters.[101] COL George A. Lincoln was a military planner.[102] COL Charles H. Bonesteel III served as an Assistant for National Security Council Affairs, Department of Defense, and would become a defense member on the NSC Planning Board after June 1953. COL Bonesteel would later command a Division, Corps and Army as well

---

[98]Ibid., 362.

[99]*Foreign Relations of the United States,* 1952-54, Vol. II, *National Security Affairs*, List of Persons, XX and 350. Kennan, George F., Ambassador in the Soviet Union, May 14, 1952 – September 19, 1952; Retired Foreign Service, Political Planner and Russian expert.

[100]Ibid., List of Persons, XXVI. Wood, C. Tyler, United Nations Command Economic Coordinator (Seoul, Korea), Foreign Operations Administration, 1953-1954.

[101]Ibid., List of Persons, XXIV. Smith, H. Page, RADM, USN (Captain until 1953), Military planner and expert on Foreign Military Matters.

[102]Ibid., 53. George A. Lincoln, USA; Military planner and economist. Head of USMA social science department from 1954 – 1969; later General; Director of the Office of Emergency Preparedness and National Security Council member, 1969 – 1973. COL George was so respected and thought of by his peers that a book of collective essays was published in his honor. The book includes essays from President Eisenhower, General Bonesteel and Lieutenant General Goodpaster; all three of whom participated in Project Solarium.

as work on the Army Staff.[103] Capt. H.E. Sears and John M. Maury served as the final two members. John M. Maury was a Soviet and Eastern European Intelligence expert who also worked as Chief of the Soviet Russia (SR) Division of the CIA's Division of Directorate for Plans (DDP).[104]

Task Force A analysis was to review arguments and propose programs that supported policy, which already existed. The directives for Task Force A: "(1) To maintain over a sustained period armed forces to provide for the security of the United States and to assist in the defense of vital areas of the free world; (2) To continue to assist in building up the economic and military strength and cohesion of the free world; and (3) Without materially increasing the risk of general war, to continue to exploit the vulnerabilities of the Soviets and their satellites by political, economic and psychological measures."[105]

Task Force B appointed members: United States Air Force (USAF) Major General (MG) James McCormack who was a military and political planner. MG McCormack was also an atomic weapons and new weapons expert for the Air Force.[106] John C. Campbell was a standing member of the Department of State Policy Planning Staff.[107] MG (Retired, USA) John R. Dean was a

---

[103]COL Amos A. Jordan, Jr., *Issues of National Security in the 1970's: Essays Presented to Colonel George A. Lincoln on His Sixtieth Birthday* (New York: Frederick A. Praeger), 333. Bonesteel, Charles H. III., Assistant for National Security Council Affairs, Department of Defense, and defense member on the NSC Planning Board after June, 1953; later, Commanding General for the 24th Infantry Division, the VII Corps, and the Eighth Army in Korea; Director of Special Studies in the Office of the Chief of Staff, USA; senior USA member of Military Staff Committee of the U.N.; graduate of USMA, the National War College, and Oxford University.

[104]*New York Times*, Obituaries; Maury, John M.; Central Intelligence Agency expert in Soviet and Eastern European intelligence; Assistant Secretary of State for Legislative Affairs, 1974 – 1976. Raymond L. Ghartoff, *Journey Through the Cold War: A Memoir of Containment and Coexistence* (Washington, DC: Brookings Institution Press, 2001), 64 and 111.

[105]*Foreign Relations of the United States,* 1952-54, Vol. II, *National Security Affairs*, 399.

[106]Ibid., 351. McCormack, MG James Jr., USAF; Military and Political Planner, Atomic and New Weapons Expert.

[107]Ibid., List of Persons, XVII. Campbell, John C., Member of the Policy Planning Staff, Department of State, 1953 – 1954.

military planner and Russian expert. MG (Ret.) Dean served as the Chief of the United States

Military Mission in the Soviet Union from 1943 to 1945.[108] Calvin B. Hoover was a noted

economist and professor who served with the OSS in WWII. Dr. Hoover served as Duke

University's Chairman of the Department of Economics and Dean of the Graduate School during

this period.[109] COL Elvin S. Ligon served in multiple key assignments within the National War

College during the Solarium exercise. He would eventually rise to the rank of MG in the USAF

and serve on multiple senior staffs.[110] Philip E. Mosely was a Russian and Eastern European

specialist. He served as a Political Advisor (POLAD) and was a member of the U.S. delegation in

Potsdam. He would serve with multiple organizations, including RAND.[111] James K. Penfield

was the final member of Task Force B.

---

[108]Ibid., List of Persons, XVIII and 351. Dean, John R., USA; Chief of the United States Military Mission in the Soviet Union, 1943 – 1945; Military Planner and Russian Expert.

[109]*American National Biography*, Vol. 11, 149-150. Hoover, Calvin Bryce, noted economist and professor; published *The Economic Life of Soviet Russia* in 1931; travelled to and researched economies of Germany, Italy, France, Poland, Czechoslovakia, Denmark, Sweden, Norway and Australia; considered a founder of the field of comparative economic systems; served in WW I and with OSS in WWII; President Truman awarded him the Medal of Freedom in 1947. Duke.edu. http://econ.duke.edu/about/history/individuals/calvin-bryce-hoover (accessed 18 March 20114). He was a member of Duke University faculty from 1925 until his retirement in 1966. He served as Chairman of the Department of Economics and Dean of the Graduate School from 1937 to 1966.

[110]Arlington National Cemetery website. MG Lignon, Elvin Seth Jr., Commanded 466th Bomber Group (Heavy), B-24's in the Eighth Army at Attlebridge, England. Observer to the "Baker" test at Bikini; June 1946 Air War College student. Air War College Staff August 1949 as a special project officer, director, academic staff, and special assistant to the commandant. National War College student August 1952. Joined the Director of Plans, Deputy Chief of Staff/Operations, U.S. Air Force, December 1955 served as deputy director of personnel planning, assigned as director on September 10, 1956. Appointed chief of staff, Chief Military Planning Staff, CENTO, Ankara, Turkey, in August 1961. Assigned as chief of staff, Allied Air Forces Southern Europe, Naples, Italy in July 1963. http://www.arlingtoncemetery net/esligon.htm (accessed 5 February 2014).

[111]*Russian Review*, Vol. 31, No. 2, April 1972. Mosely, Philip Edward. AB and Ph.D. from Harvard (1933). Instructed at Princeton, Union College and Cornell (1936-43). Russian and Eastern European specialist, Russian research (1930-32) and Eastern Europe (1935-36). Chief of the State Department's Division of Territorial Studies, political adviser to the U.S. Delegation at the foreign ministers' conferences (1943-46) and at the Potsdam Conference. President of the East European Fund; board member of numerous journals and institutions, such as the RAND Corporation, the Council on Foreign Relations, the Humanities Fund, the Hoover Institution, and others.

Task Force B assigned policy analysis: "(a) To complete the line now drawn in the NATO area and the Western Pacific so as to form a continuous line around the Soviet bloc beyond which the U.S. will not permit Soviet or satellite military forces to advance without general war; (b) To make clear to the Soviet rulers in an appropriate and unmistakable way that the U.S. has established and determined to carry out this policy; and (c) To reserve freedom of action, in the event of indigenous Communist seizure of power in countries on our side of the line, to take all measures necessary to re-establish a situation compatible with the security interests of the U.S. and its allies."[112]

Task Force C appointed members: Vice Admiral (VADM) Richard L. Connolly served as the Naval War College President during Project Solarium.[113] LTG Lyman L. Lemnitzer served as the U.S. Army Deputy Chief of Staff for Plans and Research while participating in the exercise. LTG Lemnitzer would eventually become the Army Chief of Staff as well as Chairman of the Joint Chiefs of Staff.[114] G.F. Reinhardt served as a foreign area expert as well as a Russian expert. Reinhardt also served as a POLAD and had worked in SHAPE.[115] Kilbourne Johnston participated in Task Force C along with COL Andrew J. Goodpaster. COL Goodpaster served as a U.S. Army Special Assistant to the Chief of Staff, Supreme Headquarters Allied Powers Europe at the time. COL Goodpaster had worked previously for General Eisenhower and would serve as

---

[112]*Foreign Relations of the United States,* 1952-54, Vol. II, *National Security Affairs*, 412.

[113]Ibid., List of Persons, XVII. Connolly, Admiral Richard L., USN, President of the Naval War College until 1953. Arlington National Cemetery Website; Admiral Connolly served in WWI and WWII, was awarded the Navy Cross for actions saving the U.S.S. West Bridge in August, 1916; Admiral Connolly and wife are buried at Arlington, VA., resulting from an American Airlines jet crash in New York, 1962.

[114]Ibid., List of Persons, XV-XXVI. Lemnitzer, LTG Lyman L., USA (MG until August 1, 1952), served as Commander, 11th Airborne Division, 1950 and 7th Infantry Division, November, 1951; Deputy Chief of Staff for Plans and Research, United States Army, after August 1, 1952; Chief of Staff of the Army, July, 1957; Chairman of the Joint Chiefs of Staff, October 1, 1960 – September 30, 1962; Supreme Allied Commander of NATO, 1963 – 1969.

[115]Ibid., List of Persons, XXIII. Reinhardt, G. Frederich, Counselor of Embassy in France; Foreign Relations, 1952 – 1954, Vol. 2, 351.; Foreign Service, Russian Expert, Political Advisor, SHAPE.

an aide to President Eisenhower. He was considered a brilliant military planner and with extensive background in international affairs.[116] Leslie S. Brady was a Foreign Service Officer who had served as a counselor for cultural affairs in the U.S. Embassy in Moscow.[117] COL Harold K. Johnson who served as 3-8 CAV commander up to the defense of the Pusan Perimeter. COL Johnson served as the Chief of Joint War Plans Branch during the Solarium exercise. He then served as the Assistant to the Chief of the Plans Division, and finally as the Executive Officer of the Assistant Chief of Staff prior to departing the Pentagon.[118]

Task Force C directives for analysis: "(a) To increase efforts to disturb and weaken the Soviet bloc and to accelerate the consolidation and strengthening of the free world to enable it to assume the greater risks involved; (b) To create the maximum disruption and popular resistance throughout the Soviet Bloc."[119] Task Force C is frequently referred to as the "rollback" option and aligns with Nitze's argument as part of NSC 68. Additionally, specified under paragraph 4

---

[116]Ibid., List of Persons, XIX. Goodpaster, COL Andrew J., USA, Special Assistant to the Chief of Staff, Supreme Headquarters Allied Powers Europe, 1952–1954; Staff Secretary to the President after October 10, 1954, *Foreign Relations of the United States,* 1952-54, Vol. II, *National Security Affairs*, 351; USA, brilliant Military Planner, extensive background in international affairs. COL Amos A. Jordan, Jr.; *Issues of National Security in the 1970's: Essays Presented to Colonel George A. Lincoln on His Sixtieth Birthday* (New York: Frederick A. Praeger), 334. Earlier served as Special Assistant to the Chairman, JCS; Defense Liaison Officer and Staff Secretary to the President of the United States (1954-61); achieved rank of LTG; served as Commandant of the National War College. B.S. from USMA and an M.A., M.S.E., and Ph.D. from Princeton University.

[117]*Highbeam Research, Washington Post*, Obituaries, September 11, 1992. Brady, Leslie Snowden. Foreign Service Officer with U.S. Information Agency, counselor for cultural affairs in the U.S. Embassy, Moscow; Public Affairs officer for U.S. Embassy, Paris. Served in Office of War information in WWII. http://www.highbeam.com/doc/1P2-1024578 html (accessed 6 February 2014).

[118]*New York Times*, Obituaries, September 26, 1983; General Johnson, Harold Keith. USA, USMA class of 1933; Bataan Death March survivor, released in 1945; Commanded 3-8 CAV prior to the Pusan Defense in the Korean War; attended the National War College in 1952. After graduation, Johnson was assigned to the Office of the Assistant Chief of Staff, G3, where he served first, as Chief of Joint War Plans Branch, then as the Assistant to the Chief of the Plans Division, and finally as the Executive Officer of the Assistant Chief of Staff; Chief of Staff of the Central Army Group of NATO's ground forces in 1958 as brigadier general; head of Command and General Staff College in 1960; Army Chief of Staff, 1964–68. http://www.nytimes.com/1983/09/26/obituaries/army-gen-harold-k-johnson-chief-of-staff-from-1964-to-68.html (accessed 4 February 2014). See also, Lewis Sorley, *Honorable Warrior, General Harold K. Johnson and the Ethics of Command* (Lawrence, KS: University Press of Kansas, 1998), 112-113.

[119]*Foreign Relations of the United States,* 1952-54, Vol. II, *National Security Affairs*, 416.

instructions to Task Force C, Basic U.S. Objectives there is unique commentary, "Instead of preventing "significant expansion" of Soviet Bloc power (NSC 153/1), the alternative is categorical as to preventing *any* further expansion. In reducing Soviet power this alternative calls for, "without, *however, initiating* general war" instead of the stipulation of "without *unduly risking* a general war" of NSC 153/1."[120]

Task force members were also carefully screened and ultimately approved by President Eisenhower. Member selection was crafted to ensure that the correct subject matter experts were placed on the Task Force that most accurately reflected their special knowledge base. COL Goodpaster was specifically placed on Task Force C by Eisenhower. Eisenhower desired Goodpaster on Task Force C because, "he wanted the rollback option thoroughly evaluated, and he said he wanted somebody with common sense...on Task Force C to see that they didn't go completely off on their analysis."[121] Additionally there were two other noteworthy individuals who did and did not participate in the Solarium exercise. Paul Nitze, the creator of NSC 68/2 had been nominated to participate with Task Force A. Nitze declined to participate due to "other commitments."[122] George F. Kennan, who would later become an ambassador, was not initially selected to participate in the Solarium project, but "it is likely that Eisenhower, who respected Kennan greatly" ensured that Kennan share a part of this collaborative effort. General Goodpaster elaborated further, "The President did not take part in the deliberations, but he did recommend participants: it was he who suggested that Kennan chair Task Force A."[123]

---

[120]Ibid., 417.

[121]"Project Solarium: A Collective Oral History with General Andrew J. Goodpaster, Robert R. Bowie, and Ambassador George F. Kennan," February 27, 1988, *Princeton University*, Princeton, New Jersey; Andrew J. Goodpaster, "Organizing the White House," in Kenneth W. Thompson, ed., *The Eisenhower Presidency: Eleven Intimate Perspectives of Dwight D. Eisenhower* (Lanham, MD, 1984), 71.

[122]Per telephone conversation between Dulles and Cutler, June 1, 1953, "June 1953 (telephone calls)." Chronological Series, Dulles Papers, DDEL.

[123]Pickett, 4.

Solarium Task Force Reports

Task Force A Analysis

Task Force A (TF A) accounts for the NSC 68 strategy through discussion of NSC 153/1.

The group thought that the highlighted strategies provided by NSC 153/1 were sufficient for the

United States to transition towards a "strategic offensive" phase. The NSC 153/1 policy however

was not a "perfect solution" by any means and that there was room for continued refinement and

enhanced effectiveness. The Task Force noted in its report that "there are areas in which

significant improvements could be made within the framework of 153/1."[124] The report

articulated the pursued strategy would "give the greatest assurance as against other possible

alternatives for the successful disintegration of the Soviet threat without recourse to general war,

and without increasing the risk of general war."[125] The TF report conveyed a purpose of

steadfastness for diplomatic, information, military and economic aspects. The TF sought to avoid

mistakes associated with World War I and World War II, which the U.S. and the rest of the free

world could use to its advantage over the Communist Bloc. The TF reported, "Time can be used

to the advantage of the free world; if we can build up and maintain the strength of the free world

during a period of years, Soviet power will deteriorate or relatively decline to a point which no

longer constitutes a threat to the security of the United States and to world peace."[126] Task Force

A recommended "that the U.S. government continued to reject any policy based on acceptance of

---

[124]Memorandum for the National Security Council, Project Solarium, July 22, 1953, 1. White House Office of the Special Assistant for National Security Affairs Records (WHOSANSA), DDEL.

[125]Ibid., 1.

[126]Memorandum for the National Security Council, Project Solarium, July 22, 1953, 1. WHOSANSA, DDEL.

a calculated risk of general war, as being full of risk, empty of calculation, and unwarrantedly hazardous to the continued existence of the U.S."[127]

Task Force A centered its focus on Europe. The TF analysis believed Europe to be the most critical and valuable to the interests and values of America. Analysis of the Soviet threat stated, "Soviet predominance in eastern and central Europe makes impossible a restoration of normal conditions of full stability to Europe as a whole."[128] A strong, vitalized, and cohesive free Europe, oriented toward the same general objectives as the United States would be a most important, if not decisive, factor in the successful resolution of the Soviet threat.[129]

Germany was identified as a critical component to the reunification of Europe and stability of Europe. "Our problems in Europe divide themselves, in the estimate of Task Force A, into two categories. …The most important of these are the future of Germany."[130] The TF recommended unification of Germany. German unification, "if effectively handled" could provide an opportunity to "exploit and intensify present Soviet internal stresses and achieve, in due course the first major rollback of Soviet hegemony over Eastern Europe."[131] Rearmament of West Germany (minus control of nuclear weapons) as a means to the ultimate goal of reunification of Germany, TF A argued would induce Soviets to seek immediate negotiations. German rearmament benefits would be a psychological one to the West while "increasing the stresses, strains and dangers within the Soviet Orbit."[132] Another recommendation highlighted the

---

[127]A Report to the National Security Council, Task Force A, Project Solarium, July 16, 1953, 22. White House Office for National Security Council Staff (WHONSCS), Dwight. D Eisenhower Library.

[128]Memorandum for the National Security Council, Project Solarium, July 22, 1953, 2. WHOSANSA, DDEL.

[129]A Report to the National Security Council, Task Force A, Project Solarium, July 16, 1953, 83. WHONSCS, DDEL.

[130]Ibid., 86.

[131]Ibid.

[132]Ibid., 86-89.

removal of foreign forces from West German territory. This action would demonstrate Western resolve for a peaceful reunification, diminish the threat of a surprise attack, articulate and encourage East German desires for unification and pressure the Soviets for peaceful German consolidation. TF A articulated the strength of the proposal since it "would be a negotiating position on our part which does not confront the Soviets with such excessive and impossible demands as to make their discussion out of the question."[133]

Task Force A addressed economic opportunity between the West and the Soviet Union as a means to reduce economic ties favoring the Russian republic and the dependencies of the satellite countries on the Russians. Economic engagement and reduction of trade barriers for basic commodities in the Soviet bloc countries would enable the United States to "demonstrate the falseness of Soviet propaganda which claims the U.S. is dictating in this field to our allies and is responsible for an iron curtain of its own on trade."[134] The report noted this as "an opportunity to call the Russian's bluff on trade."[135]

Economic analysis and assessment of the U.S. economy produced a confident outlook. The team looked at capacity to support a sustained security program. There would be a period of growth in the military industry to meet the initial security challenges. The team expected a decline in military expenditures over time in relationship to the gross national product. "TF A concludes that there is no question that our country has the economic capacity to provide a high plateau preparedness – certainly the program envisioned by TF A – over a sustained period."[136] Analysis determined that the standard of living would improve barring any significant economic disruption. Economic resources could be dedicated and sustained against the communist threat.

---

[133]Ibid., 90.

[134]Ibid., 77-78.

[135]Ibid., 79.

[136]Ibid., 54.

The task force investigated the national debt and the impact of taxes and revenue on a sustained security program. The team's conclusion: "Our Task Force is convinced that the United States can spend more than now contemplated, if necessary, and still maintain over an indefinite sustained period a sound, healthy, free enterprise economy. The United States can and should reduce the deficits in the annual budgets, should not have a policy of operating continuously on an unbalanced budget, and should achieve those objectives by paying more taxes as we go forward in this age of danger…The United States can afford to survive."[137]

Task Force A articulated the emphasis of policy towards Europe and illustrated concern towards the Far East. The analysis mentioned that the United States had lost prestige and that non-European peoples had a decrease in favorable opinion about the U.S. The team acknowledged that much of the loss of prestige was a combination of dealing with a Communist China, the Korean War and the Korean War Armistice discussions at the time. "Nevertheless, we are compelled to recognize that, in the opinion of our Task Force, the United States has lost importantly in prestige in Asia vis-à-vis the Chinese Communists as a result of the Korean War."[138] Task Force A recommended that policy refer to China as hostile to the U.S. and until China could be separated or "detached" from Moscow. The recommendation reaffirmed that until the Korean War and the conflict in Indo-China were resolved there should be no change in policy towards China.[139]

---

[137]Ibid., 54.

[138]Ibid., 111.

[139]Ibid., 112-114.

Task Force B Analysis

Task Force B derived its policy as a unilateral policy as a method of approach within a broader context of a policy of containment.[140] The United States would have to make it unequivocally clear to the Soviet Union that further aggression and expansion would be intolerable and paramount to initiating a general war with the free world. TF B determined a clearly articulated message to the Soviet leadership with the main new policy emphasis on "The warning of general war as the primary sanction against further Soviet-Bloc aggression."[141] The TF argued that by specifying to the Soviets that their aggressive actions would serve as a precursor for general war this policy would generate the greatest opportunity for a long period of peace. TF B stated "General war is defined as a war in which the U.S., assisted by those allies it might have at the time, would apply its full power – whenever, however and wherever necessary to defeat the main enemy, and to achieve its other war objectives" with a predicted effect that "a clear indication that further military aggression by the Soviet Bloc would result immediately in general war will reduce the likelihood that such a war will occur."[142]

Task Force B's group report articulated in the preface that the report was simply an analysis of a directed course of action. "In conference with the directive we have presented our best advocacy of the policy assigned to us for analysis. We believe that Alternative "B" does merit serious consideration as a basic element in U.S. foreign policy. Otherwise, in the nature of the assignment, the members of "Task Force B" do not assume personal responsibility for the conclusions expressed."[143] This disclaimer is interesting to note as some have argued that the

---

[140]A Report to the National Security Council, Task Force B, Project Solarium, July 16, 1953, 19. WHONSCS, DDEL.

[141]Ibid., 19.

[142]Ibid., 20-21.

[143]Ibid., Preface.

reason for this is "In part because Task Force B lacked an advocate who, like Kennan, was intimately familiar with and deeply committed to its charge."[144]

The Task Force B analysis of the policy of containment resulted in a challenge for the team to determine what "line" might generate conflict. There were "gaps" identified, mainly as the Middle East and South Asia. The recommendation of the Task Force was that "this gap should be closed by a line along the present Soviet Bloc periphery" in order of assuring that all other free countries would not be seen as opportunities for inclusion under communist control.[145] The TF reasoned that the policy would be more effective discouraging Soviet aggression everywhere by prohibiting Soviet aggression anywhere.

Task Force B analysis concluded that a period of atomic plenty would be achieved by the Soviet Union. The TF did not articulate that when the period of Soviet atomic aplenty arrived that it would constitute conflict. Task Force B elaborated, "The growth of the Soviet stockpile is inevitable, but not the creation of the conditions prerequisite to its employment."[146] The team believed that unless preemptive war was initiated to prevent the Soviets from reaching atomic plenty that the clear declaration and delineation of what would generate a response from Soviet aggression was almost certain to help guarantee greater stability or chance of enduring peace. "The warning of general war as the primary sanction against further Soviet-Bloc aggression, under clearly defined circumstances is the best means available for insuring the security of the United States, for the present and the foreseeable future."[147] The reduction of peripheral war was reduced through clarity of a declared policy of a chance of the Soviet Union from "stumbling"

---

[144]Bowie and Immerman, 131.

[145]A Report to the National Security Council, Task Force B, Project Solarium, July 16, 1953, 7. WHONSCS, DDEL.

[146]Ibid., 12.

[147]Ibid., 2-3.

into a general war, "It diminishes to the vanishing point the probability the U.S.S.R. will either deliberately initiate or blunder into a general war."[148]

The team believed that within COA B that there would be a period in which Soviet policy would adjust or refine its actions in policies. Because of the clearly articulated policy of COA B the TF believed that the Soviets would be induced to change over time and that Soviet leadership could not indefinitely sustain undue hardship on their citizens. The TF elaborated, "It would require the indefinite and unrelenting maintenance of present Soviet psychological pressures. These pressures are based on a remnant of revolutionary enthusiasm grown stale after 35 years even within the top leadership and on the aftermath of defensive counter-offensive national upsurge…Over time, these psychological factors, at present favorable to Soviet purposes, will lose their force."[149] The Task Force believed that it would be wrong to view the Soviet system as completely inflexible. They argued the Soviet policy could change over time with the result of expansionist desires subsiding. TF B stated, "Finally, it is in the realm of the possibility that the U.S.S.R. will gradually relinquish the active and increasingly risky pursuit of its program of world expansion. In the past Soviet leadership has shown considerable flexibility in adjusting its immediate goals to changes in real and recognized power situations."[150]

Additional weight for Task Force B centered on the concept that U.S. containment policy would immediately draw or use allies as a proxy for conflict against the Soviets or their Bloc countries. U.S. leadership would galvanize allies through employment of the policy. The Task Force remarked, "It will make clear that the U.S. does not hire others to fight its wars for it, and will provide a firmer basis for U.S. relations with other Free World countries."[151] TF B argued

---

[148]Ibid., 43.

[149]Ibid., 82.

[150]Ibid.

[151]Ibid., 13.

that the course of action enhanced support to allies while undercutting Soviet propaganda that allies were proxies for U.S. policies. The team elaborated further, "Alternative B will undercut the suspicion, widely propagated abroad, that the U.S. aim in supporting regional defense pacts is to 'get other people to fight its battles'."[152]

Task Force B stated from an economic perspective, "Our proposed policy will help stabilize the economy of the Free World, by stabilizing the cost of defense and providing a confident political atmosphere for economic development."[153] The TF argued that clearly announced defense policy enhanced economic conditions with the reduction of the potential for peripheral conflict. Their report remarked, "Removal of the threat of piecemeal Soviet aggression would enable the United States to employ its resources most effectively for national and Free World security and to maintain its economic position over the long-term in the face of growing Soviet economic power."[154] A supporting economic aspect to the paragraph above with regards to the U.S. using "other people to fight its battles" the TF supported the plan as effective by "The elimination of peripheral wars would also rob the Soviet leaders of the advantage they now possess in being able to use the resources of a satellite such as China in war against the United States while conserving Russian resources."[155]

Task Force C Analysis

Task Force C was charged with analyzing their directed course of action as a "roll back" perspective. Task Force C's report was the longest of the three directed COAs. The Task Force analyzed the COA through a perspective of three periods; the Near period consisted of the 1st five years, from 1953-58. The Mid period took a perspective of seven years beyond the short period,

---

[152]Ibid., 59-60.

[153]Ibid., 20.

[154]Ibid., 74.

[155]Ibid., 76-77.

from 1958-65. Finally, the Long period was considered beyond the Mid-term with no set terminus.[156] The team evaluated the directed "roll back" utilizing the following frames: Political, Military, Economic, Propaganda and Covert Operations.[157] TF C did not describe the "Long Term" period in great detail or analysis but stated, "Below these 'objectives of current action' there should be a stratus of mid-term and long-term aims, less limited in nature, posing a deeper challenge to the U.S.S.R., concealed from public disclosure and, to the maximum extent possible from Soviet discernment. Longer term aims should generally guide the formulation of the short-term courses of action."[158]

TF C shared similarity with TF B as juxtaposed to Task Force A. Task Force C lacked a leader who was dedicated and passionate about the COA. The lack of a principal advocate like Kennan for Task Force A that was an expertise in the field may have reduced the full impact of the course of action analysis. The team argued strongly for their assigned COA but may have lacked the passion that Kennan brought with Task Force A. The result was that the report most likely "could only speculate about the potential benefits and outcome of the course of action it was assigned to advocate."[159] The task force projected the report through the lens of its directive and did not appear to be particularly passionate for the project assigned, "We were instructed to act as advocates of Policy C in developing our presentation and report, but to express any individual reservations or dissent considered necessary. There have proved to be no reservations of this nature on the program as a whole. Details and particulars, however, remain subject to

---

[156]A Report to the National Security Council, Task Force C, Project Solarium, July 16, 1953, 3. and chart, 68. WHONSCS, DDEL.

[157]Ibid., 81.

[158]Ibid., 88.

[159]Bowie and Immerman, 134.

further evaluation and study."[160] COL Andrew Goodpaster, per earlier discussion, was assigned to TF C by President Eisenhower because of his knowledge and expertise. His assignment to Task Force C was to ensure that the directed policy did not wander from the specified analysis. COL Goodpaster however, did not fill the "passionate director or voice" of the analysis.

TF C recommended the proposed policy because the "first and distinguishing principal is **action** – purposeful action on U.S. initiative to reduce the threat posed by the Soviet Union through weakening its power and reducing its militancy."[161] Task Force C felt that Course of Action C was the "most feasible method of obtaining our objective and, at the same time, of avoiding general war is to end the cold war. We are convinced that the only way to end the cold war is to face up to the challenge posed by the Communist conspiracy and devote the necessary effort to the task of winning the cold war."[162] As part of a directive and aggressive outlook towards engaging the Soviet Union, Task Force C even proposed to "outlaw the Communist Party in the United States."[163] TF C recommended that consistent and sustained pressure across all fronts was demanded and that the U.S. "not suspend the tempo of those hostilities or reduce military pressure on the enemy before a settlement is actually reached."[164] The group argued that "We have played it safe. Our urge to action has always been blunted by an underestimation of our own elements of strength…and that Counsels of caution have too often prevailed."[165] Ironically however there is some contradiction with the recommended policy. The Task Force admits that "while we would like to end this creeping Communist conquest of the world by crushing it with

---

[160]A Report to the National Security Council, Task Force C, Project Solarium, July 16, 1953, 1. WHONSCS, DDEL.

[161]Ibid., 85.

[162]Ibid., 8.

[163]Ibid., 22.

[164]Ibid., 23.

[165]Ibid., 77-78.

one blow, we do not now have the power to do so with sufficient certainty of success. We also found that any such approach would be tantamount to declaring a preventative war or to issuing an ultimatum – both of which were beyond our terms of reference" and the action may invite general war.[166]

Task Force C rejected the containment policies of TF A and B on premise of "Implied acceptance of the **status quo**" and that "Time has been working against us." The team argued that following the current policies has only favored the Soviets, "We have lost ground for a decade."[167] Task Force C felt that Policy C was a strong approach towards engaging the cold war through a political, economic and military lens. TF C believed Russian power was centered on the Eurasian landmass and that it was the only true threat as there was "a relative preponderance of power available to our enemy on the Eurasian land mass."[168] Proactive engagement and an aggressive stance "exploits the principal that 'nothing succeeds like success.'"[169] An aggressive posture of "roll back" could generate a great ascendancy over the Soviet Union and it would exponentially create additional problems for the Soviets and Soviet-Bloc. Task Force C argued that TF A and TF B courses of actions have been restrained and resulted with reduced the effectiveness of the desired policies. The report stated, "Task Force C believes that restrictions imposed on such courses of action have greatly limited their effectiveness. While results have been sometimes rewarding, the whole underlying philosophy is negative and defensive."[170]

Task Force C recommend activities directed against Soviet satellites to create friction with the intent of separating the satellites from the Soviet-Bloc. TF C recommended "steps

---

[166]Ibid., 80.

[167]Ibid., 10.

[168]Ibid., 75.

[169]Ibid., 19.

[170]Ibid., 74.

generally as enumerated by the NSC in peacetime courses of action – straining Soviet-Satellite relationships and disruption of Soviet power."[171] TF C envisioned the employment of the policies through all means available using militarily, economically, diplomatically, covert and propaganda to achieve success. Successful agitation between the Soviet state and the satellites would beget further agitation and strain an already strained relationship. TF C elaborated, "Successes will compound themselves by creating additional unrest and generating more uprisings in the Satellites and eventually within the various strata of the Soviet Union."[172] Task Force C also recommended Policy C successes from a Mid-term perspective. Task Force C reported, "At the end of the Mid-term or in 1965, it is envisaged that the Satellites will be freed, or in such a state of disaffection with U.S.S.R. as to constitute a serious weakness rather than strength in the Soviet Bloc."[173] To further agitate the Soviet-Satellite relationship the Task Force recommended fanning the flames of nationalism. Task Force C observed, "We note a recent tendency in the United States to criticize and play down nationalism as something undesirable. We regard this as a mistake. We believe that in many areas the forces of nationalism offer a strong and effective weapon against international Communism and Soviet ambition and should be exploited wherever possible."[174]

Task Force C recommended actions "that would isolate Communist China politically and prevent her being seated in the United Nations or any other international body. We would take every feasible mean to weaken her economy. To that end we would maintain an embargo on trade with Communist China and induce our allies to do the same."[175] Rollback would be pursued

---

[171]Ibid., 16.

[172]Ibid., 69.

[173]Ibid., 7-8.

[174]Ibid., 102-103.

[175]Ibid., 33.

aggressively with a recommendation "that forces of the Nationalist Government be employed for conducting active military operations against Chinese Communists."[176] One final aggressive act recommended towards China was to "overthrow Peiping or separate Peiping from Moscow."[177]

The Task Force C analysis of nuclear capabilities and limitations believed that "by the end of five years, our current atomic capability, while growing, will be neutralized largely by decisive stocks and delivery capabilities in the hands of the Soviet Union."[178] Task Force C accepted the National Intelligence Estimate Number (NIE) 65 that "the U.S.S.R. will have by 1955 a considerable stock pile of atomic weapons and a capability of delivering it against vital targets in the Continental United States."[179] The estimated date for the Soviet Union to achieve at least nuclear parity with the United States reflected similar discussion amongst TF A and TF B. Task Force C did not indicate an immediate action towards general war or a nuclear exchange between the United States and the U.S.S.R.

The aggressive policy of COA C expected resistance and friction with regards to allies. TF C remarked, "Alternative C will produce added strains upon our ties with allies. While not advocating a policy of "going it alone," we would be forced on occasion, after exhausting every means to secure concurrence of allies, to proceed unilaterally."[180] COA C as advocated by TF C would encourage allies where feasible, such that "we would press our allies to take every feasible action under their respective forms of government to harass their Communist parties and render them as impotent and as ineffective as possible."[181] Task Force C recognized dangers of being overly assertive or to the point of excessively aggressive where it would damage relationships.

---

[176]Ibid., 34.

[177]Ibid., 71.

[178]Ibid., 3.

[179]Ibid., 12.

[180]Ibid., 13.

[181]Ibid., 23.

Task Force C elaborated, "This more aggressive policy in the conduct of our foreign relations must never come to appear to the other members of the free world as a policy of aggression."[182] Task Force C recognized that our Allies may prefer not to carry out an aggressive policy. Pushing too hard under an aggressive policy could spell disaster if there was a complete failure. The U.S. had to remain sensitive towards on nations and their perspectives in coordinating policy with allies to reduce potential communist exploitation. The Task Force concern was, "The major result of failure would be to further the tendency on the part of our allies to oppose U.S. leadership and to open added opportunity for the Soviets to weaken cohesion of the free world and to strengthen their influence within France, Italy and probably the U.K., as well as throughout the Asiatic world."[183]

Germany is a point of significant discussion by Task Force C. The TF analyzed the strategy of both a unified Germany and an armed West Germany. TF C seized on opportunity to exploit Soviet actions by "seizing on the political and propaganda initiative. We would condemn the Soviets for exploiting the people of Eastern Germany beyond human endurance and demand the withdrawal of their forces from East Germany and the unification of Germany."[184] The proposed overall objective would be an independent and armed Germany. TF C stated another possibility as "A lesser objective would be a neutralized East Germany and a rearmed West Germany."[185]

Task Force C analyzed the economy with a result similar in assessment to Task Force A. TF C even integrated much of the economic analysis and report from TF A into their report.[186] A

---

[182]Ibid., 103.

[183]Ibid., 60-61.

[184]Ibid., 20.

[185]Ibid., 24.

[186]A Report to the National Security Council, Task Force A, Project Solarium, July 16, 1953, 44 to 56. WHONSCS, DDEL.

"roll-back" policy from an economic perspective recommended that the U.S. and Allies engage in a selective trade war. TF C remarked from an economic perspective, "We believe that damage can and should be done to the Soviet economy through the application of East-West trade on a selective basis – with maximum advantage to ourselves and minimum gain by the enemy."[187] TF C envisioned opportunity to exploit economic weaknesses and leverage sanctions, denial of maritime repair services, tariffs and other economic actions to disrupt Soviet and Soviet-Bloc economies.[188] The ultimate end-state of aggressive economic actions would "press the Soviets to formulate or revise major (economic) policies."[189] Task Force C laid out total economic costs to the U.S. in its analysis but ultimately concluded that overall the U.S. has financial and physical capacity to survive and excel. Task Force C is "supremely confident that the United States has the financial and physical capacity to provide for security without damaging social effects. This is the cheapest program in the long run for it seeks to end the cold war as quickly as possible without fighting a hot one."[190]

President Eisenhower summarized the Task Force briefs at the end of the briefings. The president displayed his gifted capability for analyzing and understanding complex problems by synthesizing and distilling the discussions quite articulately. The president thanked all of the participants for all of their labor and insight and congratulated them for their presentations. George Frost Kennan remarked that President Eisenhower, "spoke…with a mastery of the subject matter and a thoughtfulness and a penetration that were quite remarkable. I came away from it with the conviction that President Eisenhower was a much more intelligent man than he was given credit for being. But like Foster (Dulles) he didn't reveal (to the public) how discriminating

---

[187]A Report to the National Security Council, Task Force C, Project Solarium, July 16, 1953, 25-26. WHONSCS, DDEL.

[188]Ibid., 26-27.

[189]Ibid., 94.

[190]Ibid., 70.

and thoughtful a person he was, or how well he could present all these things."[191] President Eisenhower had provided the opportunity for all of the expert participants to publicly engage in a discourse to discuss the strengths and weaknesses of all courses of action while enabling him to decide how he wanted to proceed forward.

---

[191]Pickett, 4.

TRUMAN AND EISENHOWER – THE SHAPING AND EVOLUTION OF U.S. NATIONAL SECURITY

Presidents Truman and Eisenhower developed National Security Policies in different environments. Both leaders faced economic, diplomatic and military pressures that shaped their foreign policy development. The pressures produced policies now recognized as NSC 68 and NSC 162. Their experiences, their leadership styles and existing political environments during their tenures shaped how they would lead. Their actions established the foundation for how the United States would conduct itself through a challenging and frequently uncertain Cold War.

President Truman initially carried on the foreign policy legacy of his predecessor, President Franklin D. Roosevelt. President Truman's administration did not initially begin with an intent to address foreign policy. Truman's administrative focus was not solely oriented externally towards Europe and the Pacific with the cessation of hostilities from World War II. Domestic policies were gaining greater emphasis since the end of the war and the American people were oriented at home seeking relief from the demands required to support the war. President Truman initially proposed a Department of Defense budget that would not exceed $15 billion dollars for the fiscal year 1950.

President Truman did not initially articulate a desire for a foreign policy review. Instead it was his subordinates in the State Department, like Secretary of State, George C. Marshall and policy planner George F. Kennan who would initially lead the call for a policy review. President Truman was not particularly savvy with planning and preparing for policy planning and review. General Goodpaster elaborated, "Truman had had little experience with handling such matters and depended heavily on recommendations of the Policy Planning Staff of the State Department."[192] Harry S. Truman agreed to the review after he was sufficiently briefed by his staff that suggested another analysis of policy was in order. The president signed the policy

---

[192]Pickett, 11.

review on 31 January, 1950 and directed additional research into development of a thermonuclear weapon in the same directive. Truman, in this instance could be viewed as a reactive leader with regards to developing foreign policy since he waited for a recommendation from his subordinates.

NSC 68 and the recommended policy created by Nitze and the Policy Planning Staff served as a physical manifestation of the call for a policy review. NSC 68 quickly became recognized as a forceful argument for uniting and synchronizing the elements of national power to address a perceived communist threat. The discussion of the aggressiveness and the threat of communism was growing. NSC 68 was the latest policy that arrived on President Truman's desk. NSC 68 uncannily predicted aggressive Communist action in what was considered a remote spot in the world at the time.

The invasion of hostile Communist forces into South Korea on June 25, 1950 provided the justification to dramatically increase the DoD budget. The North Korean invasion provided President Truman the impetus and justification for domestically supporting a program of military expansion with the associated budget expenditures. Communist aggression at the local and regional levels heightened American and Western concerns about communist intentions. Communist militarism fueled anxiety about what their true intent was. Hostile global communist activities justified expanding fiscal resources and confirmed to many Department of State and Department of Defense leaders their suspicions and beliefs of communist's objectives world-wide. Communist actions reaffirmed many western leaders' beliefs that the U.S. and Western Europe must maintain sufficient military forces to deter further communist designs towards democratic systems of government. The expansion of military budgets and military capabilities heightened Western leaders concerns of balancing the rights of their people and maintaining a democratic society against security requirements to protect against the nefarious and insidious communist actions.

President Eisenhower approached foreign policy proactively compared to President Truman. Eisenhower campaigned on reviewing foreign policy and promised a "New Look" should he be elected into the office of the President of the United States. Eisenhower's previous jobs and experiences enabled him to campaign on and action his "New Look" proposal. Internal politics of the Republican Party and the proposed Republican foreign policy platform cemented Eisenhower's decision to run for the presidency. Republican Senator Taft's strong conservative and isolationist leanings helped Eisenhower to decide to run for the office of the president because of strong isolationist trends within the Republican Party. President Eisenhower was strongly opposed to the trend to return to post war isolationism.

President Eisenhower's previous jobs influenced his approach to national security policy. His experiences structured his perspective towards addressing challenging security problems. General Dwight D. Eisenhower's leadership positions as the Commander of European forces during World War II, the first Commander of Supreme Headquarters Allied Powers Europe (SHAPE) under the North Atlantic Treaty Organization (NATO) and Chief of Staff of the Army influenced his views of the political environment of the time. Eisenhower's experiences served him well, "Not surprisingly considering his career as a strategist, planner, and commander, Eisenhower knew both the importance – in matters concerning life or death and the destinies of nations – of getting the best possible information before deciding on a course of action and of selecting and organizing his planners in a way that increased the probability that they would help him discover the correct one."[193]

President Eisenhower inherited multiple policies that addressed the foreign policy path for the United States. The question remained to be determined if the policies were synchronized or supportive of each other. A potential danger existed of multiple policies which existed with

---

[193]Fred I. Greenstein and Richard H. Immerman, "Effective National Security Advising: Recovering the Eisenhower Legacy," *Political Science Quarterly* 115 (November 3, 2000): 337.

conflicting and self-defeating objectives. Policies that did not mutually support or enhance each other could create unnecessary problems and undesired effects. Different departments could theoretically conduct actions they believed were in accordance with the policy. Yet those very same departments could directly conflict with each other (knowingly and/or unknowingly) and negate desired policy end-states. James S. Lay proposed such a question on behalf of President Eisenhower to the National Security Council in the spring of 1953. The desire to have a comprehensive and mutually supportive strategic policy served as the spark for Project Solarium.

President Eisenhower's conversations with the Secretary of State John Dulles set the stage for organizing a detailed and thorough analysis of the national strategy at hand. That event culminated on Thursday, July 16, 1953 when the robust group met at the White House to brief and discuss the implications of their directed COA. Sixty senior leaders were present for the briefings. Unlike the development of NSC 68 with Dean Acheson, Paul Nitze and others present, the group that President Eisenhower brought together was a significantly larger group with a broader array of experiences and perspectives. The group included the following participants and members during the analysis briefing: Secretary and Under Secretary of State, Secretary and Deputy Secretary of Defense, Secretary of Treasury, the Attorney General, director of the Bureau of the Budget, Chairman of the Atomic Energy Commission, the service secretaries, the Chairman and Joint Chiefs of Staff, Director of the Central Intelligence Agency, Office of the Director for Mutual Security, Office of Defense Mobilization, as well as former members of the Secretary of State Plans and Policy Planning Staff along with prominent individual COA leaders with military and civilian leadership position seniority. All of these members participated in the briefing analyses, asked questions and provided comments for all participants to analyze, contemplate and discuss. The development and staffing by the Policy Planning Staff of Paul H. Nitze did not provide a forum for analysis and discourse in a large group, unlike the unique opportunity afforded to do so with the Project Solarium briefings.

The teams under Eisenhower's directive spent several weeks working on their projects, similar to the time and energy expended under the Policy Planning Staff team lead, Paul H. Nitze. The Eisenhower teams focused specifically on a directed COA but had the freedom to cross talk with the other COA teams. The fact that the teams could cross talk allowed for "cross-fertilization" between the groups as they analyzed various aspects with regards to their directed COAs. The team under Policy Planning Staff lead by Nitze was a single team that created and analyzed four different COAs. There is insufficient evidence to determine if one or more of the four COAs was quickly analyzed and simply discarded as a "throw-away" COA. Additionally it is difficult to determine if the group under Nitze deliberately created a "throw-away." The Eisenhower task forces expended greater energy and deeper analysis on a single course of action to gain greater appreciation and understanding of their directed COA. This was enabled with the creation of teams established to focus on one specific course of action. This detail towards a greater level of analysis by subject matter experts is a strength of the Project Solarium policy creation and analysis. The Policy Planning Staff group developed multiple policies and analyzed each policy. The Policy Planning Staff did not devote the singular focus and analysis compared to Solarium's task forces.

The atomic bomb impacted strategy from two aspects. The first issue concerning nuclear weapons actually energized the development of the thermonuclear weapon and the study of nuclear weapons under President Truman. The fact that the Soviet Union detonated a nuclear weapon significantly earlier than anticipated shifted the political landscape. The United States no longer was the sole nuclear power in the world. The Soviets could proudly proclaim to the world and to their communist allies that they mastered the secrets necessary to develop and employ a nuclear weapon, regardless of how the technology was achieved. The West was now on notice that Communist Russia no longer possessed a strictly conventional military capability. The Soviets were also a competitive economic powerhouse and challenged the free world economically. Successful nuclear detonation by the communists added further impetus to the United States. The Soviets could undermine U.S. prestige if the U.S.S.R. developed and detonated a thermonuclear weapon first. President Truman signed the directive to initiate thermonuclear weapon research along with a review of foreign policy as a result of the successful Russian nuclear detonation.

Communist detonation of a nuclear weapon marked the beginning of the end of American nuclear overmatch. The Russians initiated building their nuclear inventory. The Policy Planning Staff noted in NSC 68 that they anticipated the Russian nuclear inventory in 1954 could be the "year of maximum danger." This period was an artificial date determined by the Policy Planning Staff. The Policy Planning Staff articulated this "year of maximum danger" in NSC 68 as a point in time in which the U.S.S.R would have sufficient capacity and capability to deliver a devastating offensive surprise attack. This period is also referred to as the time of atomic plenty. The Policy Planning Staff analysis approached the nuclear issue as a capability issue by numbers. Meaning, that if the Russians had a sufficient number of nuclear weapons and capable delivery platforms then they would have a reasonable chance of successfully delivering a percentage of those weapons against the strategic targets of their choice.

The Eisenhower team had the advantage of time regarding analysis and gaining greater fidelity of the nuclear issue. The advantage to Eisenhower existed because of the time that passed between the Truman and Eisenhower administrations. Time between the administrations enabled the nuclear issue to settle. Communist Russia and the United States conducted analysis of the nuclear issue in depth and were not eager to use the weapon. President Eisenhower and the NSC analyzed offensive and defensive nuclear capabilities of the United States and the Soviet Union during this period.[194] Eisenhower did not believe in the "year of maximum danger" with regards to Soviet nuclear intentions. The Solarium task forces analyzed the nuclear issue from a perspective of atomic plenty for the U.S. and the U.S.S.R. versus Truman's Department of State Policy Planning Staff submission of a "year of maximum danger." Project Solarium provided greater analysis, understanding, appreciation and nuances of the nuclear challenge from a strategic perspective. The Policy Planning Staff compared nuclear analysis with separate discussions among nuclear experts during the State-Defense Working Group reviews. Project Solarium analysis revealed the threat of nuclear war could be effectively reduced with deliberate and careful actions. Project Solarium revealed the threat of nuclear war could be effectively reduced if the actions which would trigger general war and initiate nuclear war were clearly articulated to senior communist leaders.

Budget analysis was executed differently between the two analysis groups. NSC 68 budget analysis was initially generalized. The intent of NSC 68 was to identify the problems and articulate requirements to mitigate the Soviet advantage of the sustained military program expansion. Secretary of State Dean Acheson stated it most clearly,

> NSC 68 lacked, as submitted, any section discussing costs. This was not an oversight. To have attempted on would have made impossible all those concurrences and prevented any recommendation to the President. It would have raised at once the extent and tempo of the program deemed necessary to carry out the conclusions and recommendations. Each department, each service, and each individual would have become a special pleader or an assistant President weighing all the needs of the nation and the political problems presented by each need. Our function was to get the international situation analyzed, the problems it presented stated, and recommendations made.[195]

After preliminary study, the President on the twelfth asked the Joint Chiefs to have cost estimates made. While this was being done with due deliberation, the paper was discussed with the

---

[194]For greater detail and analysis, reference Memorandum by Paul H. Nitze and Carlton Savage of Policy Planning Staff, May 6, 1953, Continental Defense, *Foreign Relations of the United States,* 1952-54, Vol. II, *National Security Affairs*, 307-18.

[195]Acheson, 364.

President in the National Security Council on April 25. The policy became recognized as NSC 68.

Deliberately analyzing policy that did not initially conduct detailed budgetary analysis meant that the budget would not be considered as effectively while analyzing the problem and developing a policy according to Secretary of State Acheson. Secretary of State Acheson stated,

> While NSC 68 did not contain cost estimates that did not mean we had not discussed them. To carry through the sort of rearmament and rehabilitation-of-forces program that we recommended, at the rate we thought necessary, for ourselves and with help for our allies, would require, our group estimated, a military budget of the magnitude of about fifty billion dollars per annum. This was a rough guess…It seemed better to begin this process by facing the broad facts, trends, and probabilities before getting lost in budgetary intricacies. If that begins before an administration has decided what it *wants* to do, or made what diplomats used to call a decision "in principle" – in essence – the mice in the Budget Bureau would nibble to death the will to decide.[196]

Acheson recognized the realities of the political atmosphere and understood there would still be a necessary salesmanship required in selling NSC 68 to Congress and to the American people. Secretary of State Acheson stated, "As Oliver Wendell Holmes, Jr., has wisely said, there are times when 'we need education in the obvious more than the investigation of the obscure.' The purpose of NSC 68 was to so bludgeon the mass mind of 'top government' that not only could the President make a decision but that the decision could be carried out."[197] Acheson acknowledged he had to inform the public as to why this new policy was critical to the average American,

> The task of a public officer seeking to explain and gain support for a major policy is not that of a writer of a doctoral thesis. Qualification must give way to simplicity of statement, nicety and nuance to bluntness, almost brutality, in carrying home a point…In the State Department we used to discuss how much time that mythical 'average American citizen' put in each day listening, reading, and arguing about the world outside his own country. Assuming a man or a woman with a fair education, a family, and a job in or out of the house, it seemed to us that ten minutes a day would be a high average. If this were anywhere near right, points to be understandable had to be clear. If we made our points

---

[196]Ibid., 377.

[197]Ibid., 374.

clearer than truth, we did not differ from most other educators and could hardly do otherwise.[198]

The Project Solarium analysis brief included very senior Treasury Department leaders. The Treasury Department experts were afforded the opportunity to raise budgetary issues. Additionally they could address significant concerns in the immediate context of the briefings for all to analyze and discuss openly without external pressures.

The budget analysis conducted by the three Project Solarium teams was done so in greater detail earlier in the analytical process when contrasted with the budgeting analysis of NSC 68. Budget analysis was discussed during the initial conversation between Eisenhower, Dulles and others on the day that Project Solarium was conceived. President Eisenhower remarked that fiscal analysis was part of the larger analysis in his conversation, "and then when the teams are prepared, each should put on in some White House room, with maps, charts, all the basic supporting figures and estimates, just what each alternative would mean in terms of goal, risk, cost in money and men and world relations."[199] Special Assistant Secretary Robert Cutler also directed financial analysis as part of the Solarium exercise. The May 9, 1953 Memorandum for the Record by the Special Assistant to the Presidents for National Security Affairs states in paragraph 2.a.: The terms of reference should include directions to seek out all the factors that would go into planning a major campaign: forces needed; costs in manpower, dollars, casualties, world relations.[200]

Task Force A provided significant detailed economic analysis as part of its presentation justifying the prescribed course of action. The economic analysis of TF A was also employed by TF C in their economic analysis. Task Force C independently arrived at the same economic

---

[198]Ibid., 375.

[199]Bowie and Immerman, 125.

[200]*Foreign Relations of the United States*, 1952-54, Vol. II, *National Security Affairs*, 323.

conclusion as Task Force A while using the same economic data. Each task force independently determined that the United States could economically sustain a growth of military expenditures in support of expanding military capability.

External expertise and analysis occurred at different times in the development of the policy papers. NSC 68 was provided for further analysis and discussion to outside consultants at four different periods prior to presentation to President Truman. The State-Defense Policy Review Group served as the review forum with the external consultants. The consultants included individuals who served at premier Ivy League institutions of Harvard and Princeton. Consultant experiences varied. Several consultants served on the Committee of the United States Atomic Energy Commission. One consultant had significant financial experience as a banker (not to mention Paul Nitze's previous experiences) as well as experience working within the Defense Department (Deputy Secretary of Defense and Assistant Secretary of War for Air). External influences during the exercise of Project Solarium was limited to influences internal to the groups. There were discussions between Solarium Task Forces addressing various topics. The fiscal analysis conducted by Task Force A shared their economic data with Task Force C. Task Force C utilized the same data as Task Force A yet independently arrived at a similar fiscal conclusion. Task Force C determined the U.S. economy was more than capable of fiscally supporting and sustaining an expanded budget as a course of action. Finally, all of the Project Solarium participants collectively participated in the group conference discussing their analysis and recommendations to the President. The Task Forces could have taken comments from the briefings to further refine their analysis and recommendations based on the collective discussion. Those refinements would have then been integrated and passed forward to the National Security Council for review, discussion, refinement and approval.

The presentation of proposed policy information, conclusions and recommendations drawn from analysis were presented in a manner conducive to the leadership styles of each president. President Truman received NSC 68 after it had been staffed by the Policy Planning Staff and coordinated with external "experts" during the State-Defense Review Group. President Truman did not conduct his analysis in a forum conducive to analysis with a large group of experts. An opportunity was lost in which a significant number of experts could openly discuss and debate the pros and cons of the proposed policy recommendation with the president present. President Truman missed potential opportunities to hear new ideas, thoughts and reasoning. Instead, the President reviewed the proposed policy. President Truman forwarded his questions and concerns to be addressed by the National Security Council. President Truman directed further analysis by the National Security Council to evaluate and provide recommend actions. President Eisenhower received the briefing analysis in a different forum with a much different perspective. President Eisenhower, "desired that the exercise bring together some of the best thinkers and most experienced individuals to explore dispassionately and free from public scrutiny and comment the three most feasible approaches for the desired policy outcome. The final product needed to be a kind of debate in which participants in their preparation had access to each other and to the best intelligence available. Then, gathered in one big room, they could argue their positions before an audience of those responsible for carrying out policy."[201]

The Project Solarium exercise initiated by President Eisenhower was a unique and powerful opportunity for some of the most powerful and respected experts and analysts to gather. Project Solarium exercise offered an incredible venue for experts to openly discuss and share analysis, thoughts and opinions concerning issues which impacted or influenced national strategy and security. This was a very special moment in the history of policy development, debate and analysis in the United States. The exercise afforded a unique opportunity in which seasoned experts could gather in a secluded location free of public scrutiny to analyze and debate issues in

---

[201]Pickett, 11-12.

great detail. The experts could share in discussions or "cross-talk" complex issues amongst a large group of experts. Additionally, the teams were provided access to classified and detailed information that many or most policy makers within government as a whole may not be able to utilize or analyze to due to restricted access.

Project Solarium facilitated the research and discussions of expert analysts since they were "protected or excused" from the requirements of their day jobs or occupations. This cloak of protection enabled them to focus. The participants had the intellectual freedom to explore all the various avenues and options. The fact that the teams were shielded from distraction enhanced their abilities to focus on the assigned task at hand and search for creative solutions and answers. This intellectual freedom in turn enabled greater analysis of extremely complex problems. Finally, the ability to brief and exchange thoughts and ideas openly with a collective body of senior national leaders and experts from across the various elements of national power and government was a very privileged opportunity. The execution of the brief in a secure location open to all panel members and briefers that was free of external influences provided a powerful opportunity to explore and potentially arrive at optimal solutions for a national strategy. Project Solarium was a unique, effective and short-lived experience when compared to government planning and operations in general.

The recommendations of NSC 68 and NSC 162 have similarities. Ironically and despite the manner in which the two policies were developed the recommendations of both policies had similar aspects. NSC 68 and NSC 162 called for an expansion of military capabilities. NSC 68 recommended dynamic and immediate growth while NSC 162 called for deliberately sustained and steady growth over a longer period of time. NSC 68 and NSC 162 both recognized and discussed the budgetary impact of expanded growth and capability. Both policies identified that the American economy could absorb significant amounts of fiscal expenditure without damaging or destroying the economic future of America. NSC 68 and NSC 162 both recognize the importance of political will and the need to balance security with the rights of the individual. Leaders involved with both policies articulated the concern of violating freedoms and losing the very sacred rights of the individual for the sake of ensuring a secure future. Both policies recognized the power of a free and democratic society and the potential to effectively apply this power over time to defeat an oppressive socialist state. NSC 68 and NSC 162 sought application of all the forms of power against the Soviets and communism, one path was an accelerated option while the other was analyzed to determine what could be sustained for a long haul to change Soviet behaviors.

CONCLUSION

NSC 68 and NSC 162 were created to address recognized and perceived policy challenges. One of the primary challenges for the United States and the free world was determining a consistent national strategy following World War II. Communism behavior and aggression (real or perceived) provided additional impetus for the national leadership to determine how to reasonably and consistently respond to communist actions worldwide. NSC 68 served as a policy wake-up call to the challenge being posed by communist aggression. The development of NSC 68 and NSC 162 served to address communism with other aggressive state behaviors into a political, economic and military context that could be understood. The evolution of these policies served as a framework to guide the United States to systematically engage leaders and states world-wide with a consistent political, economic, and military policy. The framework effects sought desired international behavioral norms without increasing the potential for conventional or nuclear war.

NSC 68 was initiated as a result of a frank discussion between Department of State senior leadership and President Truman. President Truman initiated a national strategic review simultaneously with scientific thermonuclear weapons research and exploration. NSC 68 remained closely guarded within a tight group of policy experts at Department of State and Defense along with senior level White House executive leaders. President Truman did not spend significant time addressing the challenges and issues associated with developing the policy. Instead, he deferred to his subordinate experts to provide him recommendations during policy development. NSC 68 recommended economic actions with significant budget implications, contrary to President Truman's initial national economic policies, goals and projections. The successful North Korean surprise attack against South Korea on 25 June 1950 reaffirmed the suspicions of senior policy makers about communist actions and policies. NSC 68 had served a purpose of alerting the U.S. about assertive communist designs. The surprise attack by

Communist North Korea against Capitalist South Korea lent additional credence to the prognostication of NSC 68's creators. The North Korean surprise attack reaffirmed the analysis of NSC 68. NSC 68 would be implemented as policy even though the document remained classified until the 1970s.

NSC 68 was initially developed by a single working group. The State Department-Department of Defense working group was less than twenty people at any one point and included several key leaders with significant experience in the State and Defense Departments. Paul Henry Nitze was the definitive and dominant personality responsible for the creation of NSC 68. Nitze has been consistently identified as the leader and point man for the creation of NSC 68 throughout his distinguished career. Nitze served as an unfatiguable proponent to argue on behalf of the policy. Nitze observed NSC 68 successfully become policy through his tenure as the Policy Planning Staff Director.

The State-Defense Policy Review Group introduced their proposed document to several prominent leaders after the creation of the basic policy for external expert analysis and discussion. These reviews with external experts and leaders gave additional analysis and insight for discussion and consideration for the review group. The review groups enabled the creator of NSC 68, Paul H. Nitze additional perspectives to prepare for justifying, endorsing and ultimately seeking approval for NSC 68 recommendations. These staffing and review actions conducted prior to submission to President Truman strengthened the arguments for recommending approval of NSC 68.

NSC 162 was created in a different manner. President Eisenhower, along with his Secretary of State, Central Intelligence Agency Director and other senior leaders conducted an informal meeting discussing policy and Communism in the White House. The participants discussed several courses of action to address United States security and policy. The idea was floated to conduct a policy analysis of the proposed courses of action by several teams of experts and experienced leaders. The President and his leaders/advisors wanted to analyze the courses of action within the context of current U.S. policy and develop long-term objectives for the United States. President Eisenhower issued directions as to whom would participate on the teams, later identified as Task Force A, B and C respectively. The teams analyzed each course of action within the political, economic and military context to determine a suitable, feasible and acceptable plan for sustaining attainment of long-term objectives. President Eisenhower did not participate in the Task Force internal analyses but participated with everyone during the final analysis brief. The analysis briefings included everyone who participated in the Project Solarium exercise. The task force analysis provided the intellectual rigor to justify the proposed course of action. President Eisenhower summarized each of the task forces analysis at the conclusion of the briefs. The president issued additional guidance of how he wanted the policy to evolve based on the presentation analysis and discussion. The president let the leadership below him refine the product to be forwarded to the National Security Council for analysis and recommendation.

NSC 162 would eventually become the product of the directed course of action analyzed and recommended by Task Force A. The Task Forces had prominent members who were widely known, respected and experts in their fields. The leader of Task Force A, George Kennan, who had previously served at Department of State and was the predecessor of Paul H. Nitze, was the driving force leading Task Force A analysis. George Kennan served as the same energetic leader and voice of reason for the directed course of action. Kennan shaped and sold the analysis the day the task forces convened to brief President Eisenhower, senior governmental and military leaders along with the other task force team participants. Regardless of how vocal a proponent Kennan was he was by no means the only professional and expert on the teams. The assembled teams were gifted leaders and experts. Many of these experts and leaders continued to serve in positions of greater authority and responsibility within the Department of State, Department of Defense, the U.S. government and academia as a whole. These gifted experts provided the intellectual analysis that President Eisenhower desired. Their analysis enabled the president to make a deliberate and well-informed decision. If President Eisenhower had a desired course of action, he never told any of the Task Force teams. Their analysis and intellectual rigor would have enabled President Eisenhower to confirm or deny his own assessment.

The second point of the Project Solarium exercise was that the exercise was unique for policy development. Project Solarium was the first time where multiple competitive teams of experts were assembled to analyze proposed policy in great detail. The task forces were sourced by experts, provided any and all materials and references necessary for detailed analysis. The experts were protected from distractions associated with their normal "day jobs." The result was that the Project Solarium exercise provided a detailed and vigorous analysis of three separate and independent courses of action. Additionally, the Solarium exercise reflected the experiences and insights of a former Army Chief of Staff and War Plans Directorate, President Eisenhower. Project Solarium potentially confirmed what President Eisenhower had already conceived as the desired way forward. The exercise undoubtedly provided the additional logic and rigorous analysis necessary to reaffirm his suspicions. The analysis provided President Eisenhower with sufficient legitimacy necessary to execute his desired policy.

A subject matter this study did not address is talent management. President Eisenhower and his staff did a superb job of ensuring that the appropriate subject matter experts were identified and integrated into the analysis teams. Every member who participated on the Task Force teams was an expert and was recognized for their unique knowledge and perspective of the topic for analysis. Many of these members continued on to have their own incredible histories and influences. TF members went on to be prominent diplomatic, military and economic leaders, teachers and advisors. The ability of the President and his senior advisors to select "a few fine fellows" speaks to a system or pool that manages current and rising talent. This topic could be an insightful project for further academic research into how talent is managed in civilian and military circles.

NSC 68 and NSC 162 are known policies within government security circles. NSC 68 was recognized across many academic and military circles. NSC 162 did not appear to be as easily identifiable or recognized policy. NSC 162 still has elements classified. There may be many reasons for why NSC 162 is not as recognized but the question still remains: why is NSC 68 more prevalent compared to NSC 162? NSC 162 deserves further academic and historical study and analysis. The fact that Project Solarium is not widely known for creating NSC 162 should be a catalyst for greater study under Department of State and Department of Defense policy and planning groups.

Comparison of the creation and analysis of NSC 68 and NSC 162 serves as a unique exercise and informative opportunity for insight into the creation and development of national strategy and policy. These policies were created by two completely separate and distinct methods. The policies were influenced by powerful and eloquent leaders, advocates and an experienced analytical president. Project Solarium produced greater detailed analysis for a recommended policy. Did one method of analysis ultimately produce a better policy or course of action? In the end there may be no true way to determine if one method of policy development was truly greater or more effective. Another Project Solarium exercise is worthy of execution. A second Project Solarium may determine and produce the next optimal, viable and coherent long-term policy for the United States as the nation journeys into the 21st Century.

Ultimately though, the policies of NSC 68 and NSC 162 were proven effective on a cold day on November 9, 1989. One of the most recognizable symbols of Communist oppression and tyranny, the Berlin Wall, came crashing down in East Berlin, Germany. American policy along with compelling and enduring political, economic, social and military will combined with powers of the free world facilitated the demise and collapse of communist Russia and discredited

communism in world history.

APPENDIX

"12 Security Questions" from Robert Cutler, reference *Foreign Relations of the United States, 1952-54*, Vol. II, *National Security Affairs*, 230-31.

1. How far can we reduce Soviet power and influence without accepting grave risks of general war?

2. If we continue to contain Soviet power and build free world strength, will an unbearable stalemate ensue?

3. Can we reduce Soviet power and influence without deliberate subversion behind the iron curtain?

4. Do existing policies sufficiently weigh or consider the vulnerabilities of the Kremlin regime (such as indigestive results of swallowing such large areas and populations so rapidly), or the psychological aspects related thereto?

5. Should we support any government, even though totalitarian, provided only that it is independent of Soviet control and influence: or should we work only with "democratic groups"?

6. Under existing policies and programs will we ever be strong enough to negotiate a lasting agreement? What are the conditions, short of unconditional surrender, on which we would settle? Is there any acceptable temporary accommodation short of ultimate settlement?

7. Can the free world with U.S. leadership, develop an international trade and financial pattern which will eliminate the necessity for U.S. aide or for trade with the Soviet bloc?

8. Despite our offensive capability, are we carrying out adequate programs for defense against atomic attack?

9. In case of general war what conditions, if any, should be placed upon the use of atomic weapons? Under what circumstances, short of general war, might atomic weapons be employed?

10. Do we still believe that the Soviets shun war?
    a. Because they believe they can gain their ends otherwise?
    b. Because of retaliatory power?

11. Should we devote additional resources to carry out our existing policies effectively?

12. Should we reallocate our existing resources among the various security programs? How?

BIBLIOGRAPHY

Acheson, Dean. *Present at the Creation, My Years in the State Department*. New York: W.W. Norton and Company, Inc., 1969.

Adams, Valerie L. *Eisenhower's Fine Group of Fellows: Crafting a National Security Policy to Uphold the Great Equation*. New York: Lexington Books, 2006.

American National Biography. New York: Oxford University Press, 1999.

Arlington National Cemetery website. http://www.arlingtoncemetery.net/esligon.html (accessed 5 February 2014).

Beck, Nathaniel. "The Illusion of Cycles in International Relations." *International Studies Quarterly* 35, no. 4 (December 1991): 455-476.

Binder, L. James. *Lemnitzer, A Soldier for His Time*. Washington, DC: 1997.

Bowie, Robert H. and Richard H. Immerman. *Waging Peace: How Eisenhower Shaped an Enduring Cold War Strategy*. New York: Oxford University Press.

Callahan, David. *Dangerous Capabilities, Paul Nitze and the Cold War*. New York: Harper Collins Publishers, 1990.

Chandler, Alfred D., Jr., and Louis Galamos Jr. *The Papers of Dwight D. Eisenhower*. Baltimore, MD, 1970.

Cutler, Robert, and John F. Dulles, conversation. Per telephone conversation between Dulles and Cutler, June 1, 1953, "June 1953 (telephone calls)." Chronological Series, Dulles Papers Eisenhower Library.

Cutler, Robert. *No Time for Rest*. Boston: Little, Brown and Company, 1966.

Dallek, Robert. *Harry S. Truman*. New York: Times Books, 2008.

Drew, S. Nelson. *NSC 68: Forging the Strategy of Containment with Analyses by Paul H. Nitze*. Washington, DC: National Defense University, 1994.

Duke.edu. http://econ.duke.edu/about/history/individuals/calvin-bryce-hoover (accessed 18 March 2014).

Eisenhower, Dwight D. *At Ease: Stories I Tell to Friends*. New York: Garden City, 1967.

Eisenhower, Dwight D. "Inaugural Address," January 20, 1953. Online by Gerhard Peters and John T. Woolley, *The American Presidency Project*. http://www.presidency.ucsb.edu/ws/?pid=9600 (accessed 22 January 2014).

Foreign Relations of the United States, 1950, Volume I, *National Security Affairs; Foreign Economic Policy*. http://digicoll.library.wisc.edu/cgi-bin/FRUS/FRUS-idx?type=header&id=FRUS.FRUS1950v01 (accessed 15 September 2013).

Foreign Relations of the United States, 1952-54, Volume II, *National Security Affairs*. http://digicoll.library.wisc.edu/cgi-bin/FRUS/FRUS-idx?type=article&did=FRUS.FRUS195254v02p1.i0002&id=FRUS.FRUS195254v02p1&isize=M (accessed 27 September 2013).

Foreign Relations of the United States, 1952-54, Volume II, *National Security Affairs*, 323-28; Cutler Memorandum for Smith, May 15, 1953, lot 66D148, Secretary of State-National Security Council.

Gaddis, John Lewis., *Strategies of Containment, A Critical Appraisal of Postwar American National Security Policy*. New York: Oxford University Press, 1982.

————. *The Long Peace, Inquiries into the History of the Cold War*. New York: Oxford University Press, 1987.

Ghartoff, Raymond L. *Journey Through the Cold War: A Memoir of Containment and Coexistence*. Washington, DC: Brookings Institution Press, 2001.

Greenstein, Fred I., and Richard H. Immerman, "Effective National Security Advising: Recovering the Eisenhower Legacy," *Political Science Quarterly* 115 (November 3, 2000): 335-345.

Goodpaster, Andrew J., General. Oral History Interview for the Dwight D. Eisenhower Library, 1982.

Hayes, John Earl, Harvey Klehr, and Alexander Vassiliev. *Spies The Rise and Fall of the KGB in America*. New Haven: Yale University Press, 2009.

Hornblum, Allen M. *The Invisible Harry Gold, The Man Who Gave the Soviets the Atom Bomb*. New Haven: Yale University Press, 2010.

Huntington, Samuel P. *The Common Defense*. New York: Columbia University Press, 1961.

Institute for Advanced Studies. http://www.ias.edu/people/kennan (accessed 20 March 2014).

Jacoby, Susan. *Alger Hiss and the Battle for History*. New Haven: Yale University Press, 2009.

Jones, Grant W. "Education of the Supreme Commander: The Theoretical Underpinnings of Eisenhower's Strategy in Europe, 1944-45," *War and Society*, 30, no. 2 (August 2011): 109-133.

Jordan, COL Amos A. Jordan, Jr. *Issues of National Security in the 1970's: Essays Presented to Colonel George A. Lincoln on His Sixtieth Birthday*. New York: Frederick A. Praeger, 1967.

Kennan, George F. *Memoirs: 1925-1950*, Vol 1. Boston: Little, Brown, and Company, 1967.

————. Speech to the National Defense Committee of the Chamber of Commerce of the United States, January 23, 1947, enclosed in Keenan to Dean Acheson, August 21, 1950, Dean Acheson Papers, Box 65, "Memoranda of Conversations, August, 1950," Harry S. Truman Library.

Leffler, Melvyn P. *A Preponderance of Power. National Security, The Truman Administration, and the Cold War*. Stanford, CA: Stanford University Press, 1992.

May, Ernest R. *American Cold War Strategy: Interpreting NSC-68*. New York: Bedford Books of St. Martin's Press, 1993.

Memorandum for the National Security Council, Project Solarium, July 22, 1953. White House Office of the Special Assistant for National Security Affairs Records (WHOSANSA), Dwight D. Eisenhower Library.

Murphy, Charles J.V. "The Eisenhower Shift: Part I," *Fortune* (January 1956): 83-87.

The New York Times, 17 October 1948. Harry S. Truman, White House news conference, 16 October 1948.

Nitze, Paul H. *From Hiroshima to Glasnost, At the Center of Decision, A Memoir*. New York: Grove Weidenfeld, 1989.

Nitze, Paul H. Testimony of Paul H. Nitze, June 17, 1960, in U.S. Congress, Senate Committee on Government Operations, Subcommittee on National Policy Machinery, *Hearings: Organizing for National Security: The Department of State, The Policy Planning Staff, and the National Security Council,* 86 Cong., 2d sess., Washington, DC: U.S. Government Printing Office, 1960.

NSC 20/1, "U.S. Objectives with Respect to Russia," August 18, 1948 in Thomas H. Etzold and John Lewis Gaddis, eds., *Containment: Documents on American Policy and Strategy, 1945-1950* (New York: 1978).

NSC 20/4, "U.S. Objectives with Respect to the U.S.S.R. to Counter Soviet Threats to U.S. Security." *Foreign Relations*: Novermber 23, 1948: Vol. 1.

Pickett, William B. "George F. Kennan and the Origins of Eisenhower's New Look, an Oral History of Project Solarium" *Princeton University*, 2004.

Pogue, Forrest. Interview with George C. Marshall, tape 19, recorded on 20 November 1956. http://www marshallfoundation.org/library/pogue.html (accessed 19 March 2014).

"Project Solarium: A Collective Oral History with General Andrew J. Goodpaster, Robert R. Bowie, and Ambassador George F. Kennan," February 27, 1988, *Princeton University*, Princeton, NJ; Andrew J. Goodpaster, "Organizing the White House," in Kenneth W. Thompson, ed., *The Eisenhower Presidency: Eleven Intimate Perspectives of Dwight D. Eisenhower* (Lanham, MD, 1984).

Rearden, Steven L. *The Evolution of American Strategic Doctrine, Paul H. Nitze and the Soviet Challenge.* Richmond, VA: Johns Hopkins Foreign Policy Institute, School of Advanced International Studies, 1984.

A Report to the National Security Council, Task Force A, Project Solarium, July 16, 1953. White House Office for National Security Affairs Records (WHONSCS), Dwight D. Eisenhower Library.

A Report to the National Security Council, Task Force A, Project Solarium, July 16, 1953. WHONSCS, Dwight D. Eisenhower Library.

A Report to the National Security Council, Task Force B, Project Solarium, July 16, 1953. WHONSCS, Dwight D. Eisenhower Library.

A Report to the National Security Council, Task Force C, Project Solarium, July 16, 1953. WHONSCS, Dwight D. Eisenhower Library.

Russian Review 31, no. 2 (April 1972). The Editors and Board of Trustees of the Russian Review, published by Wiley, Philip E. Mosely, 1905-1972.

Security Council, 86 Cong., 2d sess., Washington, D.C: U.S. Government Printing Office, 1960.

Sorley, Lewis. *Honorable Warrior, General Harold K. Johnson and the Ethics of Command.* Lawrence: University Press of Kansas, 1998.

U.S. Department of State, Office of the Historian. http://history.state.gov/departmenthistory/people/rusk-david-dean (accessed 5 February 2014).

U.S. Department of State, Office of the Historian. http://history.state.gov/departmenthistory/people/marshall-george-catlett (accessed 17 December 2013).

Wells, Samuel F., Jr. "Sounding the Tocsin: NSC 68 and the Soviet Threat," *International Security*, 4, no. 2 (Fall 1979): 116-158.

Williams, Robert C. *Klaus Fuchs, Atom Spy*. Cambridge, MA: Harvard University Press, 1987.